Girls' Ministry Handbook

Starting and Growing
a Girls' Ministry in Your Church

Jimmie L. Davis

D1607637

LifeWay Press®
Nashville, TN

©2007 by Jimmie Davis.
Published by LifeWay Press®

ISBN: 1-4158-5263-4

Dewey Decimal Classification Number: 259.23
Subject Heading: TEENAGE GIRLS \ CHURCH WORK WITH TEENAGERS \ GIRLS

Printed in the United States of America

Student Ministry Publishing
LifeWay Church Resources
One LifeWay Plaza
Nashville, Tennessee 37234-0174

We believe the Bible has God for its author; salvation for its end; and truth, without any mixture of error,
for its matter and that all Scripture is totally true and trustworthy.
The 2000 statement of *The Baptist Faith and Message* is our doctrinal guideline.

The names and characterizations in this book are fictional,
although based on real events. Any similarities between the stories
and real people are unintended and purely coincidental.

Contents

About Jimmie L. Davis 4

A Note to Church Staff Members 5

Chapter 1: Why Begin a Girls' Ministry? 7

Chapter 2: What Are the Needs of Teen Girls? 17

Chapter 3: What is Girls' Ministry? 31

Chapter 4: A Team Approach to Girls' Ministry 45

Chapter 5: Developing and Training Leadership 55

Chapter 6: Small Group Discipleship & Mentoring 67

Chapter 7: Special Events for Teenage Girls 91

Chapter 8: Counseling Issues with Teen Girls 113

Chapter 9: Ministry to Parents of Teen Girls 143

Conclusion: Principles for a Successful Girls' Ministry 163

Additional Books & Resources 167

Notes 171

About Jimmie L. Davis

JIMMIE DAVIS attended Converse College and has the degree of Advanced Certificate in Women's Ministry from New Orleans Baptist Theological Seminary. Jimmie serves on the student ministry team of First Baptist Church, Spartanburg, South Carolina, as the director of girls' ministries. Jimmie trains women to lead girls' ministries in churches across America. She is the author of *Virtual You!,* a fun, interactive book focused on the unique needs of teen girls.

Jimmie worked alongside her husband, Sam Davis, in youth ministry for 25 years. Sam is now the associate pastor at First Baptist Church in Spartanburg, South Carolina. Sam and Jimmie have a grown son and daughter, a wonderful son-in-law, a beautiful little granddaughter, and identical twin grandsons. Her favorite pastimes are traveling and spending time with her family.

🌿 Dedication 🌿

To all the women who have a heart for raising teenage girls to be godly women.

To the men in my life for their love, support, and prayers in this ministry:
Sam, my dedicated husband for 34 years
Jordan, my son, you are a joy in my life.
Derek, God's gift to our family as our son-in-law.
Kyle and Kade, I'm trying to raise up godly young women for you to marry, boys!

To Ginger, my daughter, who has been my little girl:
My companion in ministry, my friend, but most of all, a godly woman who has taught me great things about girls' ministry.

And especially Kendall, my granddaughter:
May God pour out His blessings on you, and may He put many godly women in your life to raise you up to be a leader in the new generation of women!

But most of all to my Lord and Savior Jesus Christ for all He has done in my life.

A Note to Church Staff Members

A COMMMON QUESTION I am asked is, "Who should be responsible for girls' ministry?" It is a valid and important question to consider. Many churches choose to place girls' ministry under the supervision of the student minister or women's ministry coordinator. Girls' ministry fits effectively under either area. Many times the youth minister and the women's ministry coordinator choose to work together in meeting the needs of teenage girls. If your church decides to adopt this model of co-leadership, your church will need to determine who is ultimately responsible for this area of ministry. Regardless of under whose umbrella of responsibility it lies, girls' ministry should fit into the overall picture and vision of the church. It cannot be a stand-alone ministry and must come under the supervision of the staff person assigned to it. In smaller churches, girls' ministry will come under the authority and supervision of the pastor, even though a volunteer will directly coordinate the ministry. This presents a unique challenge for pastors who have little knowledge or background in ministering to this unique age group. To deal with this issue, a wise pastor is willing to allow the women in his church to attend conferences or other training venues necessary to equip them in ministering to girls in the church.

It will also be important for you to work with volunteers to set up and cast the vision for girls' ministry. Choose a woman or team of women who will set goals for this ministry under the direction and authority of the staff member who is responsible for this area of ministry. The more volunteers who understand the purpose and vision, the greater the opportunity for outreach and ministry that you will have. You cannot effectively minister to teen girls without volunteers! From this core group of volunteers, you will need to recruit the director or co-director. Begin to pray consistently for the person who should hold this position. Ask God to reveal to you whom He has chosen to carry out this important role. God may put this ministry on the heart of a woman in your church, and she may approach you with the vision. The staff person will guide and provide resources to equip the director to carry out her specific duties.

A special note to male staff and ministers: I applaud you for accepting the challenge of meeting the unique needs of teenage girls! You can be a godly influence in their lives, but you need the help of women in your church to show them how to be godly women. May God bless you, keep His hand on you, enlarge your territory, and keep evil from you all the days of your life!

Why Begin
a Girls' Ministry?

SEVERAL YEARS AGO, God touched my heart, and I felt a clear calling to train women to minister to the needs of teen girls. During 25 years of working beside my husband in youth ministry, I began to see a gender-neutral or male-dominant trend developing in curriculum. Many "churched" girls were no different than girls who were unchurched. Many were at risk for unsafe behaviors and often fell through the cracks of our ministry. As I searched for resources, I found very few written specifically for the needs of teen girls. God gave me the opportunity to travel to many churches, consult with girls and women regarding the needs of teen girls, and develop an intentional, organized plan for girls' ministry.

I receive requests on a weekly basis from youth ministers, women's ministry leaders, and mothers asking for information on girls' ministry. It is exciting to see that resources are being developed, girls' conferences are popping up across the country, and churches are stepping out and ministering to the needs of teen girls. Women's ministry has exploded across America over the past decade, and I believe God is calling women to step up to the plate and pass down a godly heritage to teen girls.

As I have watched the lives of many teen girls over the years, I have been fascinated with one young woman's life. I have seen documentaries about her on television and have read many articles on her life, and I have come to understand that her desperate need to be loved and accepted transcends time, culture, and personality. Let's consider her story as told by Charles Montaldo:

"Lynette Alice 'Squeaky' Fromme was born in Santa Monica, California, on October 22, 1948, to Helen and William Fromme. Her mother was a homemaker, and her father worked as an aeronautical engineer. Lynette was the oldest of three children and was one of the star performers in a children's dance troop called the Westchester Lariats. The troop was so talented that they performed around the country and appeared on the Lawrence Welk show and at the White House.

During Lyn's junior high years, she was a member of the Athenian Honor Society and the Girls Athletic Club. Her home life, however, was miserable. Her tyrannical father often berated her for minor things. In high school Lyn became rebellious and began drinking and taking drugs. After barely graduating, she left home and moved in and out with different people. Her father put a halt to her gypsy lifestyle and insisted she return home. She moved back and attended El Camino Junior College. After a ferocious argument with her father over the definition of a word, Lyn packed her bags and left home for the final time. She ended up at Venice Beach where she soon met a man. The two talked at length and Lyn found Charlie captivating as he spoke of his beliefs and his feelings about life. The intellectual connection between the two was strong, and when he invited Lyn to join him...to travel the country, Lyn quickly agreed."[1]

Deep in the soul of every woman, regardless of age, culture, or personality, is buried a need to be loved and nurtured.

The man's name was Charles Manson, the crazed leader of the Manson Family Cult, whose followers committed mass murders at his command. After Squeaky attempted an assassination on President Gerald Ford's life, she was asked in an interview why she committed her life to Charles Manson. Her answer was plain and simple, "I decided when I was 14 years old that whoever loved me first could have my life."[2] Lynette had always been somewhat eccentric and rebellious, but deep down she had a need to be loved unconditionally. She needed a place to belong and be accepted and feel important. Charles Manson gave her that place.

Times have changed. Our society and culture are different than in Lyn's teen years, but the same needs still echo in the secret places of the hearts of many teenage girls today. Deep in the soul of every woman, regardless of age, culture, or personality, is buried a need to be loved and nurtured—a need that breaks through and blossoms at an early age.

There are thousands of girls like Squeaky in our world who are looking for a person who will love them. Many girls will latch on to the first person who shows them attention, be it the drug dealer down the street, the gang leader at school, or a godly woman who will teach them about God's love. Teen girls need a place to be loved, to belong, and to be accepted unconditionally.

Why is it important to begin a girls' ministry in your church? Youth ministers or church staff often question the need for a specific ministry to teen girls because a youth ministry for both genders already exists and sometimes thrives in a local church. Is that not enough? What about Sunday School and youth trips? Can the needs of teen girls not be met through existing programs? Many of the needs of teenage boys and girls are the same. However, many of those needs must be met in gender-specific ways. Let's look at a few of the reasons it is important to have a ministry specifically for teen girls.

The Needs Are Great

In today's world, the church must have an intentional, organized plan to reach and enrich the lives of teen girls. Consider the following statistics:

- ❋ One million teens in the United States will become pregnant over the next twelve months.[3]
- ❋ Eating disorders are now the third most common chronic illness in adolescent girls.[4]
- ❋ One in three girls has had sex by age 16; two out of three girls has had sex by age 18.[5]
- ❋ Almost 35 percent of girls in high school have felt sad or hopeless almost every day for at least two weeks.[6]
- ❋ Almost 40 percent of date rape victims are between the ages of 14 and 17.[7]
- ❋ About 1 out of 10 young people self-mutilate.
- ❋ A 2006 status report from Georgetown University's Center on Alcohol Marketing and Youth "noted an increase in binge drinking among girls, who are more likely to consume hard liquor than their beer-inclined male counterparts."[8]

Churches are beginning to recognize those unique needs and are answering the call. The following profiles mirror many of the teen girls who walk into our churches on a regular basis.

MICHELLE was heavily involved in the party scene. She was accepted by the wrong crowd and attended parties characterized by underage drinking, drugs, and "hooking up" (better known in past generations as one night stands). She felt guilty for her immoral behavior, but she plunged deeper and deeper into that sinful lifestyle. She just didn't know how to get out of it. At school she felt like part of the in crowd. It met a need left unfulfilled at home. Michelle's parents were divorced, and her mom worked long hours. Her dad had been abusive, and she had a deep hatred for him in her heart. She hooked up with guys at parties, but they only used her to meet their own sexual desires. The assault on her heart by men left her deeply wounded and distrustful.

Her unhealthy relationships with teen girls started out at a party where she was dared to kiss another girl. Soon she realized that she felt emotionally attached to one specific girl, and the relationship grew more involved as the weeks passed. They would spend hours on the computer sending IMs (instant messages) to each other until late into the night. They would text message each other on their cell phones all during the day, and they cuddled in the evenings while watching TV or hanging out. In Michelle's eyes, this girl was her soul mate. Michelle's mom began to notice her unhealthy attachment to this girl and accused her of being a lesbian. Michelle did not consider herself a lesbian, but wondered if her own mother saw it in her, then maybe she really was! She knew her relationship was wrong, but it was like an addiction. The other girl had a much stronger personality. Every time Michelle suggested they back off, the manipulation would start.

A girl at school invited Michelle to her youth group, but every time she attended, Michelle was reminded of her sin. One day she heard the youth minister talk about beginning a girls' ministry. Desperate for a way out of her situation, Michelle attended the girls' Bible study and soon accepted Christ. She began to grow spiritually by studying the Bible, learning to pray, and being held accountable by her adult leaders and the other girls. She learned what healthy female relationships looked like and how to forgive those who had hurt her in the past. With the help of her small group leader, she was able to back away from the unhealthy relationship. She learned how to set boundaries for her life.

Michelle recently returned from an extended mission trip and feels God is calling her into full-time missions. Her life was completely changed because of her youth minister's vision to begin a girls' ministry.

DANIELLE weighed 90 pounds and kept her eating disorder a secret for almost a year. She ate a few grapes or lettuce leaves for lunch and threw the rest in the garbage. She ate as little as possible for dinner, but when her parents insisted that she eat, she would secretly throw up. She exercised excessively and grew thinner and more unhealthy by the day. Her hair began to fall out, and her monthly periods stopped. A friend invited her to a girls-only conference where she attended an exercise and diet workshop. While there, God spoke to her heart. She realized she was in trouble physically, emotionally, and spiritually. At the commitment time during the conference, she found the courage to ask for help. With help from her parents, Danielle is now in counseling and involved in a small group at church. This group of girls holds her accountable and supports her. She still struggles with her body image but is learning to deal with her problem. Danielle's life is different because God spoke to her at a girls' conference.

KERI, an exceptionally shy but intelligent girl, attended the youth group in the church where she was raised. She usually sat alone and never felt like she really belonged. Many of the girls made fun of her at school, and her self-esteem plummeted. The girls' ministry coordinator reached out and invited her to be in a mentoring group. Although she was reluctant, she finally agreed to give it a try. The other girls in the group began to realize that Keri had a lot to offer and was a lot of fun. Keri's self-esteem began to grow, and she started reaching out to other girls through the peer mentoring group in her church. Keri recently graduated from college and is attending law school with the intentions of working in a law practice that protects religious liberties. What a drastic change!

KRISTIN grew up in the church and had a strong desire to know the Lord and live for Him. She was a leader in the youth group and had a beautiful voice. She attended church faithfully and was active in youth choir, her discipleship group, Sunday School, youth worship, and girls' ministry activities. Her leaders saw her potential, and her discipleship leader mentored her and stood beside her through her teenage years. The youth minister realized her talent and influence and used her in the band for youth worship and as a leader on mission trips. During her college years, she volunteered with the student ministry and did such a good job that they hired her as an intern. Kristin is now on staff in the student ministry and helps with girls' ministry activities. Ministry has come full circle in her life because her youth minister and discipleship leader realized her potential and developed her leadership abilities.

These profiles could fit many of the girls in your church. Their lives, along with countless others, can be changed when your church begins to focus on the needs of teen girls. God has a plan to meet those needs.

It Is God's Plan

In His Word, God has mapped out a plan to meet the needs of young women as they mature. The church must provide avenues for teen girls to be trained by older, more mature women in the faith. Younger girls need role models and examples of a life lived in a passionate pursuit of God. Male youth ministers can be spiritual influences in the lives of teenage girls, but they can never model how to be godly women. Only godly women can fulfill that role.

The church must provide avenues for teen girls to be trained by older, more mature women in the faith.

Titus 2:3-5 states that older women should mentor and teach younger women. We seldom think about these verses including teen girls, but they do! It's amazing to realize that in His wisdom, God directed Paul to write these instructions to Titus. Although these instructions are centuries old, the need for such a model of ministry is more critical in today's world than ever before. God created men and women differently, and He is aware of the needs of both genders. He knows the value of gender-specific instruction, mentoring, and accountability. Such spiritual formation may take place haphazardly through

Sunday School and discipleship groups, but ministry to teen girls must be organized, intentional, and purposeful.

Let's be honest. Activities and programming in youth ministry are often male-focused. Most youth ministers are male and can't quite envision how to meet the needs of girls in their youth group. In defense of these wonderful guys, planning this way may be a necessity since teen girls will participate in male-oriented activities (like a flag football game), but teen guys will not participate in female-focused activities (like a makeover party). When planning for events and programs to involve all the youth in your ministry, it is necessary to take this into consideration. However, it is also of paramount importance to give girls the intentional focus they need to satisfy their unique needs as young women. It's OK to use football illustrations in a Bible study and to use a military boot camp theme for a retreat, but it is important to have activities that draw the interest of girls as well.

Jesus was the master Storyteller, using illustrations from everyday life that people could identify with—water and bread, nets and fishing, sheep and shepherds. With what do teenage girls identify? Only women can really know and understand what other women like! Those things can be used to help girls relate to spiritual truths. God intends to use women in the church to train girls and pass down a godly heritage.

Much of women's ministry is spent trying to help women through crises. While some of these issues cannot be prevented, many are caused by poor instruction, training, and guidance in childhood and the teen years.

Prevention Ministry

Many women are in crisis today as a result of poor decisions made during their teenage and college years. Much of women's ministry is spent trying to help women through crises. While some of these issues cannot be prevented, many are caused by poor instruction, training, and guidance during childhood and the teen years. Women face drug and alcohol addictions, gambling addictions, divorce, problems with their children, eating disorders, domestic violence, unhealthy relationships, confusion over their sexual orientation, and much more.

Women live in bondage to personal and generational sin, and they are turning to our churches for crisis intervention. This is a compelling ministry, but what can we do to prevent these issues from becoming crises in the first place?

The church can make a difference in the lives of teen girls by guiding them in making wise decisions as they become women. We must mentor and disciple teen girls *before* their values are set, or else they may make horrible or even fatal choices. For example, if a girl doesn't receive the love and affirmation she needs at home, doesn't have a strong relationship with Jesus Christ, and is never taught purity as a lifestyle, she is at risk for falling in love with the first man who tells her he loves her, even though he may be a very poor choice for a mate. She may choose a husband who will be abusive, unfaithful, or worse. Learning to make wise decisions enables girls to look back on their lives with less regret.

It is the responsibility of parents and the church to teach young women how to make wise decisions based on the truth of God's Word.

Unfortunately, today's culture is marked by poor parenting models. Some parents have abdicated their role to the TV, the school, or even to the Church and do not take an active role in helping their children become self-sufficient. These children are often shaped and molded by whatever suits them at the moment, without a thought to the consequences of their actions. Some parents adopt an authoritarian style of parenting, raising their children by telling them what to do and what not to do but failing to teach them how to think. In both of these family systems, the children cannot make wise decisions because they have not been taught the skills they need to do so. It is the responsibility of parents and the Church to teach young women how to make wise decisions based on the truth of God's Word. As this occurs, prevention ministry will slowly overtake crisis intervention ministry.

God's Kingdom Purpose

While there are many reasons to begin a girls' ministry in your church, the bottom line is this: God has chosen to use the Church to carry His message to the world and bring people to a saving knowledge of Jesus Christ. Preteen and teen girls are important to His kingdom. Who will these girls grow up to be one day? A missionary? A lawyer? A teacher? What part will they play in God's kingdom purpose? Will they change public policy? Will they model Christlike love to inner city kids? Will they mentor a whole new generation of girls who desperately need guidance? A girls' ministry is a critical avenue through which God can change the lives of girls for His glory and kingdom.

I was shopping in the mall a few years back when a young woman ran up to me, gave me a big hug, and said, "I can't believe it's you! I remember you helped me with my hair and makeup on a retreat one time. It meant so much to me, and I felt so beautiful. I never told you, but I knew at that point that I wanted to help girls in the same way. I'm a youth minister's wife now." We talked for a few minutes as she told me what God was doing in her life. As we parted ways, I couldn't remember anything about the girl or even which church she'd attended. I was too embarrassed to ask her. To this day, I still can't remember her name. Helping her with her hair and makeup was intentional, but at that point I had no idea that God would use this girl for His kingdom. Intentional and well-planned girls' ministries can literally change the course of history in the lives of teen girls for eternity.

Intentional and well-planned girls' ministries can literally change the course of history in the lives of teen girls for eternity.

Just as important, God wants to accomplish His plan in your life. He brings younger women across your path so that you can walk with them in their relationship with God and others. In doing so, you can enjoy the thrill and satisfaction of making a difference in the life of a young woman and know the awesome privilege of being a part of God's overall kingdom plan.

Your entire church will be affected when you begin to minister to the needs of teenage girls. Parents will be more equipped to raise their daughters. Families will become stronger and healthier. And your church will become more effective in reaching others. The following chapters of this handbook are intended to equip you to accomplish the task of raising a new generation of women whose hearts follow hard after God.

CHAPTER 2

What Are the Needs of Teen Girls?

THE BASIC NEEDS OF TEEN GIRLS—love, worth, safety, purpose, hope, self-esteem, and friendship—remain the same across generational lines, but each generation faces complications that are unique to its time. The culture in which students live is always changing; therefore, the way we minster to teen girls must change as well. While the message of Jesus Christ and the truth of His Word remain timeless and powerful, the way in which we communicate that truth must change with each successive generation.

This generation battles postmodernism, an ideology founded on the belief that there is no absolute or objective truth; instead, each individual creates his or her own sense of meaning, existence, and moral code based on personal preference and experience. Postmodernism has permeated every aspect of today's culture, including education, government, movies, radio, TV, magazines, the Internet, and even religion. As a result of this create-your-own-reality mind-set, the postmodern generation can be described in four ways: experiential, participatory, image-driven, and connected.[1] Students want experience. They crave participation instead of sitting on the sidelines. They value images. And they starve for connection with others. With this critical understanding of today's teen girls as a backdrop, let's explore some key needs of teen girls.

1. To Know the Truth of God's Word—Teen girls need to know the truth of God's Word and how it applies to their lives. They need a foundation upon which to build their lives. In the past, morals governed our country and most families. These morals were based on truth from Scripture, which was understood as the authoritative guide for life. In today's culture, no such thing as absolute truth exists. Moral standards and conduct are based instead on personal

preference and tolerance of others. Less than one in three teens believe that a recognizable standard of right and wrong apply to everyone.[2] Seventy-two percent of teens believe that you can determine if something is right or wrong by whether or not it works in your life.[3] As a result, teens are saying, "Don't bore me with your rules, your values, or your belief systems. And don't tell me what to think. I'm supposed to figure out what works myself, in the real world."[4] Indeed, tolerance of everything (except traditional Judeo-Christian values), even if it is repulsive to some, is the norm of the day.

A girls' ministry must uphold and proclaim the truth set before girls, even if such a standard of truth seems unpopular or socially stigmatized.

From a developmental standpoint, postmodern ideology creates a difficult, if not impossible, situation for teen girls. They are being asked to define and live by their own standard of right and wrong without having sufficient tools to make informed, intelligent, and wise decisions that could shape the rest of their lives. Because doing anything they want is considered OK and nothing is viewed as being wrong, girls assume that all behaviors are acceptable, even though those behaviors could cause long-lasting damage physically, emotionally, socially, and even spiritually. Some girls are promiscuous, which leads to pregnancy, STDs, and other physical problems, not to mention the emotional or social ramifications. Others abuse alcohol and drugs. Some struggle with their sexual orientation. Many teen girls are caught in a downward spiral physically, emotionally, intellectually, and spiritually. To combat the effects of postmodern ideology, a girls' ministry must be biblically based; teen girls need to know that His Word is the truth. They should be challenged by Scripture and educated about women in the Bible whom God used for His kingdom. A girls' ministry must uphold and proclaim the truth set before the girls, even if such a standard of truth seems unpopular or socially stigmatized. Truth doesn't change even if the current cultural tide doesn't like it.

Girls do not necessarily want someone to give them a specific answer. They prefer to search and connect the dots in the way that makes sense to them. Because today's teens are non-linear thinkers, they need to be challenged to take God's Word and search out the answers. Teenage girls need a godly woman to encourage them in using the guidelines in God's Word to work through every-day issues. They need guidance in learning to think and discover the truth of God's Word and how it applies to their lives as women.

2. To Know Boundaries—Boundaries are almost nonexistent in today's culture. The world teaches our children that it is OK to make their own rules: "Whatever is right for me may not be right for you, and whatever is right for you may not be right for me. We can all just do whatever feels appropriate." However, research indicates that a measure of a child's success is determined in part by the existence and enforcement of boundaries. Teens desperately need to understand that some behaviors are OK and others are not.[5] Saying no to a teen is not a bad thing! Teens need to learn that some actions and attitudes are acceptable and promote their own health and well-being, as well as the health (physical and emotional) of others. Unfortunately, many parents contribute to this problem by not setting boundaries within the home. Many parents are over-committed, consumed with their jobs and their own problems, don't want to be the "bad guy," or are just too lazy to set boundaries. Setting boundaries and enforcing them takes too much time, energy, and effort. Because of the high divorce rate in America, many teens have different sets of boundaries (if any), depending on visitation and custody rights. The church must be willing to establish reasonable boundaries and challenge teen girls to live within those boundaries.

Research indicates that a measure of a child's success is determined in part by the existence and enforcement of boundaries.

Boundaries provide security. Girls may see how far they can push those boundaries, but they are actually testing to see if the boundaries are secure. In most cases, teen girls thrive under this healthy model. On the other hand, where there is no truth, there are no boundaries. Where there are no boundaries, there is no security. And in that setting, teen girls do not thrive as readily.

Girls need to understand that boundaries established in God's Word are always intended for our protection and for our good. He is not trying to make our lives miserable by giving us a bunch of do's and don'ts that strangle out any possibility of happiness or joy. On the contrary, God wants His children to experience abundant life. He wants us to avoid the consequences of poor and sinful choices that He knows will bring nothing but heartache and destruction in the end. God's love is the basis for His boundaries! As we minister to the parents of these teen girls, we must help them understand this concept as well. Boundaries are a demonstration of love for their teenage daughters.

3. To Know that God Has a Plan for Their Lives—The need to know one's purpose is universal. "Who am I?" and "Why am I here on this planet?" are fundamental questions of our existence. It is especially important for teenage girls to understand the reason for their existence. In today's egocentric culture, teens (and adults!) often succumb to the faulty mind-set that says, "It's all about me." They need to grasp the awesome truth that the God of the universe not only created them uniquely and wonderfully (Ps. 139), but He also has a plan for their lives. This understanding of God's purpose in their lives provides girls with the basis for healthy self-esteem. If given the choice, most girls would describe themselves as plain, disposable, and nondescript, much like a paper cup, rather than beautifully designed and valuable, like a hand-painted porcelain teacup. Our goal is to give teen girls a glance into the heart of God so they can begin to grasp how valuable they are to Him and that He has a purpose for their lives.

When teaching teenage girls, I often draw a time line. The beginning dot

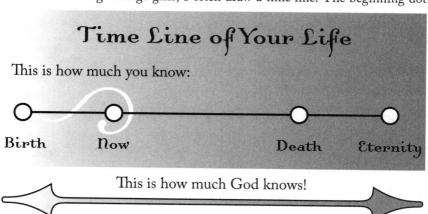

Time Line of Your Life

This is how much you know:

Birth   now   Death   Eternity

This is how much God knows!

represents their birth. The second dot represents their life now. The line continues, and the third dot represents their death. I ask them this question, "How much about your life do you know?" Of course their answer is, "From the first to the second dot." My reply is, "God knows everything from before the first dot through eternity. He has it planned specifically. Are you willing to follow Him to find your great adventure?"

Low self esteem, caused by many factors in a teenage girl's life, will deepen the feeling that God does not care about her. If God does not care about her, then certainly He cannot have a plan for her life. A purposeful plan to enrich the lives of girls will enhance their self-esteem. Girls will begin to feel that God really does care and has a specific plan for their lives, not just in the big events (marriage, family, career) but for small details of life, too (cheating, boyfriends, relating to parents).

When teens don't experience acceptance and belonging in their families, they will naturally seek acceptance in other places.

4. TO EXPERIENCE A SENSE OF FAMILY—In years past, the average family consisted of a mother, father, and children who ate meals together, attended church together, and communicated on a daily basis. The family was central. Today, the definition and shape of a family has changed dramatically. While most homes still reflect the traditional two-parent model, many other family structures continue to help shape the landscape.[6] Teen girls live in one-parent homes, live with their grandparents, live with two moms or dads (in the case of homosexual unions), or even live with non-relatives. Those families who are relatively intact spend much of their time apart, consumed in their own activities—children at sports or extracurricular activities, parents at work or pursuing their own interests. Communication often takes place through cell phone conversations, text messages, or not at all. Many girls live in homes where the mother is the custodial parent who works two or three jobs just to make ends meet financially. Many girls spend every other weekend with the noncustodial parent and don't really feel at home either place. In many churches, girls are only able to attend Sunday School and discipleship groups every other week because they are visiting their noncustodial parent the other weekend. These girls are left with few boundaries and little family structure, resulting in low self-esteem, anger, depression, emotional pain, and profound loneliness. Some families who do have a mother and father in the home are often filled with anger and conflict resulting

in emotional detachment. Sometimes the hurt is so deep they simply cannot cope with their spouse, and they detach emotionally as a coping mechanism. Parents live under the same roof for the sake of the children, but have no love between them. The children caught in the wake of this "emotional divorce" are often left without any emotional support, stability, or encouragement.

All of us as human beings have an innate longing for a place to belong and be accepted. This is especially important in the teen years, during which adolescents are struggling to find worth and autonomy simultaneously. When teens don't experience acceptance and belonging in their families, they will naturally seek acceptance in other places. Girls try to fill the need emotionally while guys seek a sense of belonging physically. Girls tend to focus on how they look and feel (consider their obsession with makeup, hair, dress, and nails), but guys focus on their physical strength, their manhood, their ability to win through sports, and other physical activities. Dating relationships, gangs, cults, gothic groups, and even cliques provide a false sense of family for teenage girls. Many girls are willing to do anything to be accepted.

Many times if a girl does not experience a sense of family at home, she will subconsciously try to create a "family" in a romantic relationship with a guy. She will first latch on to a guy emotionally and then eventually, physically. Often a girl will be haphazard in pregnancy prevention with the subconscious thought that if she has a baby, she will have a stronger sense of family. I received an e-mail recently from a girl who said she had a strong desire to have a baby. She said she would even be willing to be raped in order to have a child! She was 15 years old.

Planning time for building relationships is vital. Girls need time to talk, share feelings, and connect with other girls who are feeling the same way.

One of the growing complications of this generation is the Internet. Almost daily, news reports tell about girls seeking relationships and becoming vulnerable with strangers on the Internet. Sexual predators are capitalizing on our children as a result.

Recently, a young girl developed a relationship with a man in another country through MySpace.com. Even though she knew nothing about this man, she bought a plane ticket and flew to meet him without her mother's knowledge. This young woman was desperate for family, and she was willing to risk everything for it. The deep need for love and family clouded her judgment and put her at risk. The police found her, and she was brought home safely. Others have not been so fortunate. We will discuss more about Internet safety in the chapter devoted to parents of teen girls.

The church can provide a sense of belonging and a positive environment for these girls through mentoring groups, discipleship families, and support groups. Teaching girls to recognize their need to belong and that a relationship with the Lord Jesus Christ is the foundation for all of their other relationships is the starting point in girls' ministry. Planning time for building relationships is vital. Girls need time to talk, share feelings, and connect with other girls who are feeling the same way. Whether it is sitting on the sidelines talking while the boys play sports, having sleepovers, taking a girls' night out, or meeting as a small group, time spent making connections is important in girls' ministry.

Many teenage girls do not receive the love they need from their parents. Even if parents genuinely love their daughters, it may be hard for them to know how to demonstrate it in a healthy manner.

5. To Be Genuinely Loved—The need to be loved is a timeless, universal need, but when a teenage girl's love bank is empty for any number of reasons, the results can be disastrous. Many teenage girls do not receive the love they need from their parents. Even if parents genuinely love their daughters, it may be hard for them to know how to demonstrate it in a healthy manner. Many parents suffer from faulty family systems passed down to them from previous generations and do not have the skills or abilities to demonstrate unconditional, healthy love to their daughters. Many focus on their jobs, personal problems, or addictions and spend little time focusing on the needs of their daughters. This problem transcends socioeconomic status, class, or culture. One girl in my small group who came from a very wealthy family once said, "I've come to realize that rich people are the saddest people in the world." She was speaking from personal experience.

When they do not experience unconditional love in the home, teenage girls often look for love elsewhere. When little girls begin to transform into young women, fathers often distance themselves, and their relationship with their daughter changes. Fathers feel awkward holding their daughters on their laps or hugging them. Often girls feel that their dads no longer love them. Dads need help in knowing how to relate to their daughters as they grow into young women. Stepfathers need additional help in knowing how to relate to stepdaughters. It is difficult to know how to relate to a teenage girl who is not your own flesh and blood. Some stepfathers do very well. Others struggle, and it can even become a source of sexual temptation in their lives. Couple that with a girl's insecurity and a deep need for love, and a volatile situation emerges.

While fathers often struggle with the changing relationship with their daughter during adolescence, mothers also face a dilemma when their daughters become young women. The need for autonomy and independence causes conflict. Some teenage girls subconsciously view their moms as competition for the attention of their fathers. When mothers understand this perfectly normal feeling, they know how to better relate to their daughters.

Because of the drastic changes that take place in the family relationship, training and equipping parents to genuinely love and understand their daughters is essential in girls' ministry. Father/daughter events, mother/daughter events, parenting seminars, and marriage seminars will enhance parent/daughter relationships and communication. Even simple steps like hosting an informal meeting in which parents can discuss their struggles and frustrations can be important tools in ministry to teen girls.

Many teenage girls will jump at the first young man (or woman) who shows her attention. The need to be loved overrides good judgment.

You have probably heard the adage "looking for love in all the wrong places." To mirror the tendencies of today's teen girls, we can change that saying to "looking for love in dangerous places." Many teenage girls will jump at the first young man (or woman) who shows her attention. The need to be loved overrides good judgment, which often results in violence, STDs, and other painful consequences. In America today, a husband or boyfriend abuses a woman every nine seconds.[7] Domestic violence is at an all time high rate. Unfortunately, many of these women think they are at fault, they deserve such treatment, or they might not find love if they don't stick by the abuser.

Many young girls are willing to have sex with any guy that comes along because it makes them feel loved. In years past, that could get a girl pregnant or give her an annoying sexually transmitted disease, but today it can spell death. According to the Centers for Disease Control, from 2000 to 2004, the number of deaths due to AIDS increased among adolescents who were exposed to the disease by heterosexual contact. That same report indicated that the estimated number of AIDS cases increased at a higher rate among females than males.[8] The dangers are real, but most teens do not recognize it. Unfortunately, the church has been mostly silent about this.

Teenage girls need to know that true happiness, fulfillment, and love come from a relationship with Jesus Christ. When they receive His love and are totally secure in it, they will be ready for earthly relationships. Teaching teenage girls to set standards for their lives based on God's Word will help protect them from abusive, dangerous relationships.

Teenage girls need to know that true happiness, fulfillment, and love come from a relationship with Jesus Christ.

6. **To Fill the Need for Godly Female Role Models**—God entrusted parents to raise and guide their teens. While God designed the family to be the source of support, encouragement, guidance, and instruction, many girls do not have a godly example to follow at home. To help parents with this need, parenting classes and ministry to parents are a vital part of a church's ministry. The church comes alongside the parents to enhance the nurturing process. However, these attempts are sometimes unsuccessful in helping parents over the hurdles in their lives that will improve their relationships with their daughters. Sometimes, women in the church must teach girls how to live their lives for Christ, no matter what their circumstances are at home. Godly women can be examples for girls to follow by developing relationships, mentoring, and discipling them. Even when a girl has a godly mother modeling how to be a woman for her, it is still necessary to have other godly women in her life. Teenage girls are women and mothers in training. Girls learn how to be godly women by watching godly

women, walking alongside them, and participating in life with them. The following is a letter from a teenage girl to one youth minister's wife:

Dear Debbie,

I can't begin to thank you for all you have taught me. I have not really had a very good example to follow at home. My mom left a few years ago, and I don't really get along with my stepmother. I have watched as you take care of your children on youth trips and how you support Steve in youth ministry. I have noticed how much the two of you love each other. I have learned how to become a good mother and wife by watching you. I hope someday I might even make a good minister's wife. I know you probably didn't even know I was watching you, but thanks anyway.

Love, Heather

Debbie was shocked because she had no idea the girl was watching her. This was a wake-up call for Debbie, and she began to intentionally reach out to the young girls in the youth group. She has developed a heart for mentoring teenage girls and, with the help of her husband, started a mentoring program for girls in the youth group. You are a role model whether or not you intend to be one. Girls are watching and learning. What are you teaching them with your life?

7. **To Be Guided through the Unique Problems of Womanhood**—In the past, girls began to mature physically around the ages of 11, 12, or 13. Today, many girls are beginning to mature physically around 9 or 10, leaving a span of three to four years where they are left hanging in the gap between childhood and adolescence. Most girls will start menstrual periods around the age of 12 or 13. However, periods may start in girls as young as 8 or as old as 15 or 16 and still be considered normal.[9]

They are searching for answers and, unfortunately, are finding answers based on worldly standards.

Regardless of when it begins, the maturation process from child to young adult is filled with unique challenges that girls face. Girls are reaping the consequences of sinful lives at younger ages because they are exposed to temptation earlier in life. They are exposed to a buffet of worldly fares through the Internet, TV, movies, and their cell phones. It is difficult for parents to protect the innocence of their children because evil is everywhere. Even TV commercials are filled with dangerous messages that fill the minds of our teen girls. Consequently, their hearts become hardened earlier, making it difficult to reach them for Christ.

Girls need help in sorting through issues such as sexual and physical abuse, unwanted pregnancy, sexually transmitted diseases, hormonal issues, dating, understanding the male mind, dressing appropriately, eating disorders, self-esteem issues, friendship conflicts, family problems, spiritual issues, and the daily challenges of life as a female. I have folders full of questions from teenage girls. They are searching for answers and, unfortunately, are finding answers based on worldly standards. Girls need someone who understands, and no one understands like another female! Who but another female can understand the hormonal changes that take place each month in a girl's life? Who but another female can understand the heartbreak when a boyfriend walks away with your best friend? Who but another female can understand the insecurity a girl feels when all her friends are going to the prom, and she is the only one who doesn't have a date? Who but another female can understand the violation and shame a girl feels when she has been sexually abused or raped? Girls' ministry can provide the avenue to help girls work through the unique problems of womanhood.

Despite the information at their fingertips, teen girls often shy away from the challenge to develop intellectually. This may be due in part to the cultural standard that values external beauty more than intellectual ability.

8. To Be Challenged Intellectually—Teens today have access to more information than previous generations because of computers, the Internet, and TV. However, despite the information at their fingertips, teen girls often shy away from the challenge to develop intellectually. This may be due in part to the cultural standard that values external beauty more than intellectual ability. As a result, teen girls are less likely to be curious and are less confident in their own thoughts, feelings, and opinions. They often defer to boys and play dumb instead of demonstrating their intellectual ability for fear of intimidating boys.

Girls are ready for a challenge. They need an environment in which they can express their thoughts and opinions. They need adults who will challenge them to use their God-given intellect. They need to pursue intellectual aspects of their faith (knowing why they believe what they do) and not just emotional or relational aspects that may come more naturally to them as females.

9. To Develop Three Basic Relationships— Girls long for three basic relationships: 1.) a relationship with God; 2) relationships with significant adults; 3.) healthy peer relationships.

God created everyone, including teen girls, for a relationship with Himself. As a result, girls experience an intrinsic need for a relationship with their Creator. More often than not, they mistake this deep need in their heart for the need to have a relationship with a boyfriend or someone else who gives them a sense of security. This is a tricky area, because God also designed women to be relational. We as women often define our sense of well-being and happiness through our relationships, while men derive their sense of worth through their work or significant tasks. Nevertheless, these three areas are critical. Girls crave a relationship with God. They crave relationships with adults and relationships with peers. And if any of these areas is lacking or anemic, the overall well-being of the girl is affected.

God created everyone, including teen girls, for a relationship with Himself. As a result, girls experience an intrinsic need for a relationship with their Creator. More often than not, they mistake this deep need in their heart for the need to have a relationship with a boyfriend or someone else who gives them a sense of security.

Unfortunately, Internet relationships are replacing personal relationships. Girls sit in front of their computer, and they can be whomever they want. Using the computer, they create different versions of themselves in order to develop a sense of who they want to become as a person, which is a natural part of adolescence. In previous years, girls would try on different personalities by changing their wardrobe, makeup, and even their friends. Today, this process often takes place over the Internet, where girls can change their online persona in an instant.

Current culture does not encourage teen girls to develop a growing relationship with God, relationships with significant adults, or healthy peer relationships. Television programs geared toward young people often promote a negative attitude toward God and parents. Many times, movies give girls ideas on how to be "mean girls." Many girls think it is cool to gang up on and be mean to other girls. Many youth think it is not cool to have a good relationship with parents or other adults and often brag to their friends about confrontations with parents. Younger adolescents tend to think adults really don't like them.

Mentoring and discipleship groups will make it more comfortable for girls to build significant relationships with adults. Their friends are there, the conversation is comfortable, and they begin to see that adults really do like them. When a relationship is established between the girl and her mentor, the adult then earns the right to hold her accountable for her relationship with God. Mentoring and discipleship groups foster all of these relationships, making a happier, healthier, more well-adjusted young lady who is able to make wiser life decisions.

CHAPTER 3

What Is Girls' Ministry?

GIRLS' MINISTRY is an intentional and organized plan to meet the unique needs of teenage girls. The ultimate purpose is to spiritually transform the lives of teenage girls. Girls' ministry can be organized and carried out within the context of youth ministry or under the umbrella of women's ministry. In talking about girls' ministry, it is also important to talk about what it is not:

❀ Girls' ministry is not a stand-alone program in the church. It does not function independently from or in competition with other ministries. It must come under the approval and guidance of the pastor, the youth pastor, and/or the women's ministry coordinator. Girls' ministry must fit within the overall mission statement of the church. The goal is to carry out that mission within the context and scope of girls' ministry.

❀ Girls' ministry is not just another program to take up the time of the minister—time he or she probably doesn't have. In fact, a well-organized girls' ministry dove-tails with already existing ministries. For example, a church that organizes its discipleship groups along gender and age lines is already structured for ministry specific to teen girls. That church could use that discipleship time to allow godly women to lead a Bible study for teen girls. Within this discipleship setting, the church is training women to be involved in the lives of teenage girls and minister to their needs.

❀ Girls' ministry is not the entire solution to the needs of teen girls. Rather, it is a significant piece of the puzzle that has been missing. Girls' ministry will assist in accomplishing a more balanced student ministry and help build the kingdom of God. It is not a silver bullet or magic formula that will solve every problem teen girls face. However, it can be a strong component to effective ministry to girls.

Dimensions of Girls' Ministry

Let's face it—girls and guys are just wired differently. There are dozens upon dozens of books that describe the differences between the genders and the struggle that each gender meets in trying to understand the other. One such book written by Bill and Pam Farrel is *Men are Like Waffles, Women Are Like Spaghetti*. In it, the authors use two common foods to describe men and women. Men are like waffles:

> "If you look down at a waffle, you see a collection of boxes separated by walls. The boxes are all separate from each other and make convenient holding places. That is typically how a man processes life. Our thinking is divided up into boxes that have room for one issue and one issue only. The first issue of life goes in the first box, the second one goes in the second box, and so on. The typical man lives in one box at a time and one box only... Social scientists call this "compartmentalizing"—that is, putting life and responsibilities into different compartments."[1]

Women, on the other hand, are like spaghetti:

> "If you look at a plate of spaghetti, you notice that there are lots of individual noodles that all touch one another. If you attempted to follow one noodle around the plate, you would intersect a lot of other noodles, and you might even switch to another noodle seamlessly. That is how women face life. Every thought and issue is connected to every other thought and issue in some way. Life is much more a process for women than it is for men."[2]

In other words, one area of life affects other areas. Things are intertwined. In a similar manner, the dimensions in a girl's life—spiritual, physical, intellectual, emotional, and relational—are like strands of spaghetti. All of these areas are intertwined. If these elements of a girl's life are not balanced well, her whole life will be affected. Let's take a look at the different dimensions of ministry to teen girls. You can also look at the diagram on the next page for reference. For success in girls' ministry, we must focus on all five dimensions of a teenage girl's life. You can use this diagram as a model for your own ministry to ensure a comprehensive program that will meet the unique needs of teen girls.

A girl's relationship with God will affect every area of her life, and it is the defining factor for every other relationship in her life.

Spiritual

The foundational area of a girls' life is her relationship with God through Jesus Christ. If she has never accepted Christ's payment on the cross for her sins, then her whole life will be out of balance: her thinking will be distorted (intellectual); her emotions will be unstable (emotional); she will not value her body (physical); and her relationships will suffer (relational).

A girl's relationship with God affects every area of her life and is the defining factor for every other relationship in her life. That is why this dimension is the center of the diagram. If a girl has not allowed Christ to give her security, she may have addictions, be sexually promiscuous, believe lies from the devil, or give her heart and body away to any guy who comes along. On the other hand, if she is focused on learning about God through Bible study and prayer, attends church to grow and worship, and is growing in her relationship with Jesus, she will develop a good foundation for every other area of her life.

Every aspect of girls' ministry should have the girls' spiritual needs in mind. This does not mean that you have to do an in-depth Bible study every time you get together, but if an event conflicts with the truth of God's Word, you should question that activity. For example, an easy girls' night out for fun and fellowship is dinner and a movie. On one occasion, I allowed a student ministry intern to plan this event. She suggested a popular movie at that time. I asked if it had any negative material, and she replied, "No, I loved it. It was great!" Ten minutes into the movie, I realized it was not a movie that promoted what we were trying to teach girls spiritually. (I learned a great lesson: always preview a movie before showing it to girls!) Always ask the question, "How does this event or program meet their spiritual needs?" Make sure that everything you do—from small group discipleship to special events—lead a girl into a deeper relationship with God and give her a strong foundation for all of the other areas in her life.

Intellectual

Another area of a girls' life is the intellectual dimension. This encompasses how a girl thinks and processes what she believes, determining how she will act. Dozens of verses speak about a person's thought life. Here are a few:

"A simple man believes anything, but a prudent man gives thought to his steps."
—Proverbs 14:15 (NIV)

"Finally brothers, whatever is true, whatever is honorable, whatever is just, whatever is pure, whatever is lovely, whatever is commendable—if there is any moral excellence and if there is any praise—dwell on these things."
—Philippians 4:8

"When I was a child, I spoke like a child, I thought like a child, I reasoned like a child. When I became a man, I put aside childish things."
—1 Corinthians 13:11

"We demolish arguments and every high-minded thing that is raised up against the knowledge of God, taking every thought captive to the obedience of Christ."—2 Corinthians 10:4b-5

Suppose a young woman thinks she needs a certain young man to survive and be happy. She believes if he asks her out, she will be happy. If she believes her happiness and well-being depend on this young man, she will do anything to get him. She may become obsessed with him and spend all of her waking hours working toward the goal. She may be willing to exchange sexual favors as well as other damaging behaviors for affection just because she believes she needs him to be happy. Her thoughts led to actions that impacted every other area.

If a girl believes (intellectual) she must look a certain way (physical) to receive love and value (emotional), she will do whatever it takes to look that way. Magazines, movies, and TV use models to set an unattainable goal of perfection. Pictures of models are airbrushed to make them look flawless. Teenage girls compare themselves to the model on the cover and begin to believe they must look the same way to be loved and accepted. When a girl compares herself to others, her self-esteem is affected. She will try to dress and look exactly like the models in the magazine.

The mind is a complex machine, and when it is filled with garbage, sooner or later that faulty thinking will become evident. Have you ever noticed an unpleasant odor in your home and couldn't quite figure out where it was coming from? As the days passed, the odor became stronger and stronger until finally you were led to the source? In a similar way, when a girl fills her mind with the garbage of the world, an offensive odor will begin to emerge in her life. Her actions will bear the stench of sin, so to speak. As leaders of young girls, we must teach them to recognize truth and flee from the lies of Satan. When a girl fills her mind with the truth of God's Word, sets her standards accordingly, and lives a life of obedience, her life will be a fragrant smell to God and others.

When planning events or programs for teenage girls, make sure you are teaching truth in the Bible studies and small group sessions. Help them learn to think critically and find answers in the Bible. Girls' conferences with breakout sessions that focus on the important issues they face will be helpful in teaching girls to think through issues and learn decision-making skills in their lives.

On Wednesday nights during the summer, our church offers a guided discussion for teenage girls in our church called "Chick Chat." We choose topics the girls are interested in, and they meet together with an adult facilitator. She guides the discussion and helps the girls find biblical answers to their everyday problems. Some of the topics included: "Mean girls and how to deal with them," "Attention junkies: are you one of them?," "Being a young woman of security," "What do guys really think?," "Setting dating standards," "Personality 411," and "When God's girl prays." You could easily implement this in your own church. Just ask girls to write down topics they would like to discuss. Create an informal, safe setting so the girls know they can freely discuss without being criticized. Ask open-ended questions to promote thinking. Make sure the girls know they will always be led to the truth in God's Word in the end. How a girl thinks and what she believes affects how she feels, which leads to the emotional dimension of a girls' life.

Emotional

The third area of a girls' life is the emotional dimension. If you have ever been around teen girls, you know that their emotions can impact every other area of their lives! And true to adolescence, those emotions can swing like a pendulum in a matter of minutes. A girl's emotional state impacts her relationship with others and God and what she thinks and feels about herself. Two major influences affect a girl's emotional state. First, a girl's childhood and family environment will have a direct bearing on her emotional health. If she has been abused or neglected, she will feel emotionally unstable. Whatever generational sins have been passed down to her will also affect her emotional well-being. When a girl's love bank is empty, her emotions will be a wreck. In many instances, professional help is needed to repair and overcome the emotional damage left by physical, sexual, or verbal abuse.

Sometimes all a girl needs is another woman to sit beside her, listen, cry with her, and then at the appropriate time, have a good belly laugh!

Not only does a girl's environment affect her emotions, but the physiological changes connected with adolescence have a direct effect too. Only another woman can understand the hormonal issues a girl experiences during her growth into womanhood. Hormones affect emotions and need to be taken into consideration. Sometimes all a girl needs is another woman to sit beside her, listen, cry with her, and then at the appropriate time, have a good belly laugh! Godly mentors can meet that need.

In terms of ministry to teen girls in the area of their emotions, teaching them to guard their hearts (Prov. 4:23) is an important aspect of emotional health. Teaching a girl to guard her heart by giving it to God for safekeeping will help her to protect her emotions. She must learn to give her hurts and pain to God through prayer and a relationship with Him. When appropriate, she may open her heart to others who will love and protect her heart as well. Unfortunately, many teen girls do not guard their hearts, and as a result, they give their hearts away to men, friends, and other people who do great damage to the emotional state of teen girls. Discipleship and mentoring groups are excellent ways to build deep, healthy relationships between women and teenage girls and teach them how to guard their hearts.

Physical

The fourth area is the physical dimension. All of the other areas discussed earlier have a direct bearing on the physical dimension of a girl's life. What a girl does with her body is not only physical, but also affects her spiritually, intellectually, emotionally, and relationally. How a girl takes care of her body is affected by her relationship with the Lord, what she believes, and how she feels. Getting the right amount and kind of food, enough exercise, and adequate rest will be determined by what a girl believes. Her belief system will partly determine what harmful substances she puts into her body, such as alcohol, drugs, and tobacco. It will also impact how a girl presents herself and dresses. Does she dress attractively or seductively? Modesty is not only an intellectual and spiritual issue but also a physical issue.

Choosing purity carries a direct bearing on every aspect of a girls' life, from her social circles to her emotions. Conversely, impurity affects every area of a girl's life and can have devastating results.

38

One specific area of the physical dimension that must be addressed is purity. Setting standards for purity starts in the mind (intellectual) and is carried out in the actions (physical). Choosing purity carries a direct bearing on every aspect of a girls' life, from her social circles to her emotions. Conversely, impurity affects every area of a girl's life and can have devastating results. Most of the time a girl will give her heart (emotional) before she is willing to give her body (physical). Once she has fallen in love with a guy, it will be easy for her to fall into sexual temptation. Low self-esteem, feelings of emptiness in her heart caused by separation from God, and not basing her standards and worth on the truth of God's Word make this temptation even more appealing. For many girls, these confusing emotions and thoughts are combined with the strong need for a sense of family. The attention and false sense of love she receives during sex create a sense of family in her mind. Thus, it is vital for the church to create an ongoing dialogue about physical purity and a Love that never fails. When a girl believes this in her mind and is truly secure in her relationship with Christ, she will not be as emotionally and physically vulnerable to any guy who comes along. Teaching her to set her standards based on God's Word will help her to treasure her purity instead of giving it away as a trinket.

Of course, the physical dimension of a girl's life also deals with physical appearance. Many girls focus on their looks constantly. They compare themselves to other girls to see if they measure up, and most of the time, they come up short and desire to change how they look. This is not only a problem with teenage girls, but women as a whole. The rising numbers of women (and teen girls) who undergo plastic surgery indicate that this is an issue. The testimony of many women who have had extreme makeovers proves that outward appearance does not bring true happiness.

Girls must be taught that they are caretakers of their bodies, not owners (1 Cor. 6:19-20). They must learn to not focus solely on outward appearance (as our culture does), but they must also learn to value their body. The numbers of girls with eating disorders and who injure their bodies through cutting testify that girls wrestle in this area of self-image. We should teach teenage girls that God made them uniquely beautiful. He has a reason for the way He created them. While it is OK to want to be attractive, it is unhealthy to fixate on it to the detriment of one's health, outlook, relationships, and worth. Teaching a girl to honor God with her body is a vital ingredient in growing godly women.

The church can provide events, training, and resources to help girls in the area of purity. Girls can participate in sports together, such as a powder-puff football game or basketball tournament. Exercise and nutrition classes can teach girls how to take care of their bodies. Mother/daughter shopping trips can be used as a fun way to guide girls in choosing the proper clothes to wear. A True Love Waits emphasis in your church can guide girls to make a commitment to purity in their lives. (For more information, visit *www.truelovewaits.com*.)

Relational

A girl's relationship with the Lord Jesus Christ is the determining factor for every other relationship in her life. If she has "God-esteem" rather than self-esteem, she will interact with others more successfully. When she finds security in her relationship with Jesus Christ, she will not need to put unrealistic expectations on others. When she is growing intellectually and bases her life and standards on the truth of God's Word, she will be able to make wise decisions that foster healthy relationships. When she is taking care of her body by getting proper exercise, good nutrition, and not putting harmful substances in it, she will have more energy to invest in healthy relationships. By keeping her mind and body pure and healthy, she can gain the respect of others. When a girl's relationship with God is well-balanced and growing, she can develop and maintain proper relationships with others.

A girl's relationship with the Lord Jesus Christ is the determining factor for every other relationship in her life.

A girl's relationship with others will impact her effectiveness for the kingdom of God. For example, if a girl is sexually involved with a guy, her witness may not be taken seriously by others who know about her promiscuity. If she is using drugs or addicted to alcohol, she will not be able to be a strong witness. If she has low self-esteem, she will not have the confidence to witness or fulfill the plan God has for her life.

Another area of the relational dimension is the use of the tongue. It is a small part of the body, but it causes great harm when a girl becomes involved in gossip, slander, profanity, or just plain negative talk. Girls seem to have a deeper, more serious problem with gossip and "mean talk" than guys. Girls typically have more words and a greater need to get them out than guys do; therefore, it seems to be a greater temptation. Teaching girls to be quick to listen, slow to speak, and slow to become angry (Jas. 1:19) will enable them to develop better relationships. Modeling and accountability are the best ways to show girls how to get rid of gossip. In my small group, I had girls who were unusually prone to gossip. I set up boundaries: prayer requests must be personal and not about the garbage in another person's life; prayer requests or personal information cannot be talked about to anyone, not even to each other, after leaving the group; and negative talk about other people will not be tolerated. If the girls started to talk negatively about other girls, I would simply say, "Girls, we need to change the subject." On the other hand, if the girls knew of someone who was struggling, they knew they could come to me personally (rather than ask during a large group discussion) and ask advice on how to help the other person.

It is natural for teenage girls to have squabbles and fights, but a leader of girls must be trained in helping girls work through the everyday issues of getting along with others.

The following is a good exercise to use when teaching girls about healthy relationships. Instruct girls to listen as you name certain people. When you say the person's name, they are to say the first thing that pops into their minds. Name people that the girls will recognize, such as famous presidents, sports figures, and movie stars. Name people who have ungodly or godly reputations such as: Bill Clinton, O.J. Simpson, Janet Jackson, Billy Graham, Madonna, Britney Spears, Tiger Woods, and Mother Teresa. Point out they either had negative or positive responses toward the person. Ask, "What caused you to think negatively or positively about that person?" The answer is *their actions.* Then ask, "What would pop into a person's mind if I said your name?" This causes a girl to realize that all of the areas of her life determine her reputation. Her reputation will determine her relationships with others. Her relationship with others will determine how effective she is for the cause of Christ.

Discipleship and mentoring groups are the ideal avenue for teaching girls about relationships, but they can become a hotbed for problems! It is natural for teenage girls to have squabbles and fights, but a leader of girls must be trained in helping girls work through the everyday issues of getting along with others. Small groups can be the best way to teach girls how to love each other, accept each other, and not be jealous of each other. When small groups continue long enough to go through a few storms of life together, they will begin to learn how to develop godly relationships with others.

The Benefits of Girls' Ministry

Numerous benefits result from girls' ministry within the context of youth ministry or women's ministry:

❀ Teenage girls will accept Christ and understand that He has a plan for their lives. Many times, problems and traumatic events prevent girls from understanding how much God loves them and how He wants to be involved in their lives. When those problems and needs are addressed and girls realize that God's Word has the answer to their biggest problem (a broken relationship with God), girls will be drawn to accept Jesus Christ. They will be more likely to grasp the fact that God has a specific plan for their lives.

❀ Girls' ministry is a safety measure designed in God's Word. Building a close relationship with a teenage girl is risky for a male youth minister. Often a male student minister knows there is a need for ministry, but he does not feel equipped to handle situations with girls. The youth ministers or male youth workers will face less temptation in their relationships with girls, and they will be legally protected when an effective girls' ministry is in place. The hearts of teenage girls will be better protected against falling in love or becoming infatuated with males in ministry.

Titus 2 clearly states that women should mentor and train younger women while men should mentor and train younger men. There is a place for the spiritual influence of males in the lives of teenage girls, but specific boundaries should be set and never crossed. The guidelines in God's Word are always for our protection. Some men take lightly an innocent crush by teenage girls. There is no such thing as an innocent crush and teenage girls are always hurt when a crush is encouraged or allowed. More and more student ministers are losing their jobs, being sued, and even being incarcerated because of their sexual involvement with teenage girls in their youth groups. A wise youth minister will never get involved in close mentoring relationships with teenage girls, nor will he allow male youth workers to do so. His job is to make sure that women are continually being trained in the church to mentor and teach the young women in his youth group. My wise husband often says, "A minister is only one accusation away from being out of the ministry. It doesn't matter if the accusation is true or false, the results are often the same."

❀ The youth ministry will begin to grow numerically. When the needs of teenage girls are being met, they will talk. It's hard for girls to keep that kind of thing to themselves! When other girls hear what is going on, they will want to be involved as well. Girls stick together. They even go to the ladies' room in herds! Girls will reach out to their friends as a result of their changed lives.

❀ Your church will have a part in growing a new generation of godly women. Girls will learn to make wiser life decisions and therefore have to deal with fewer negative consequences than earlier generations. As stated earlier, much of women's ministry involves repairing the damage of past mistakes and providing healing and hope for the future. By ministering to girls, you have the opportunity to be proactive in reaching girls and moving them in a positive direction before they become broken women. The girls you minister to today will be the future leaders in our churches.

❀ Girls will be equipped to reach out and minister to their friends, drawing them into a relationship with Jesus Christ. The purpose of discipleship is for the person who is being discipled to become the discipler. In other words, the purpose of discipleship is to help young women mature as Christians and then begin to teach younger girls themselves. It doesn't matter if you are 50 years old or 15 years old, there is always a younger girl whom you can mentor. When God touches and changes the life of a teenage girl, she will naturally want to share what He has done in her life.

❀ Girls will be better prepared to become wives, mothers, and Christian women in the future. When girls are taught how to make wise decisions, set dating standards, guard their hearts, and get rid of childish ways, they will mature as Christians and be better prepared for life as a woman.

❀ You will grow stronger in your walk with the Lord. When you realize that younger girls are watching you, it will become more important to you to be dependent on the Lord for your strength. Hopefully, you will desire to be more obedient to Him and to study His Word so you can give of the outflow of God's work in your own life. As a result, you will become closer to the Lord, and you will grow stronger as a follower of Christ.

The Tasks of Girls' Ministry

Girls' ministry should exist to fill in the gaps that overall youth ministry misses in the lives of teenage girls. As discussed in chapter one, females need intentional, organized ministry. Some of the tasks of girls' ministry include:

- Meeting the unique needs of teenage girls
- Leading teenage girls to a personal relationship with Christ
- Discipling girls to become followers of Christ
- Teaching girls the Bible and how it applies to their lives as women
- Training girls in missions and evangelism
- Showing girls how to fulfill their purposes as godly young women
- Teaching girls to love their families and be submissive to their parents
- Leading girls to own their faith so when they leave the youth group they will know how to continue their Christian walk
- Leading girls to be a part of the overall church, not just the youth group
- Preparing girls for marriage, motherhood, and a profession

As we keep in mind the spiritual, intellectual, physical, emotional, and relational aspects of a girl's life, we must develop the following areas in girls' ministry in order to help accomplish our goals:

- Training women to minister to teenage girls
- Establishing mentoring and discipleship groups for teenage girls
- Staying abreast of counseling issues with teenage girls
- Planning special events for teenage girls
- Equipping parents to relate to teenage girls

Each of these components will be discussed in detail in the following chapters. Fasten your seat belts and get ready for a great adventure in the wonderful world of teenage girls!

CHAPTER 4

A Team Approach to Girls' Ministry

SOME CHURCHES are beginning to hire a staff member to focus on ministry to teenage girls, but most churches do not have the financial means to hire someone exclusively for girls' ministry. Do not be disappointed if your church falls into the latter category! There are steps you can take to organize a ministry to meet the needs of girls, regardless of the size of your church.

If you are the pastor or youth pastor and you feel God is leading your church to minister to the specific needs of teenage girls, you should pray and choose a leadership team. Many of the following steps will be carried out by the women and girls on that leadership team. If you are in a small church, your leadership team may consist of one or two women and a couple of teenage girls. In larger churches, there may be a director or girls' ministry coordinator who will work with the leadership team. The size of the team will vary according to size of the church.

In larger churches, teamwork is important when beginning a girls' ministry. Often the director of women's ministries will work alongside the youth minister to facilitate ministry to teenage girls. It is important to determine who is ultimately in charge of the girls' ministry and who will have the final authority to make decisions. The minister of education or minister to adults will need to be involved sometimes, especially when coordinating parent ministry. Whether you are serving in a small or large church, the following steps, with minor adjustments to fit your church, will be useful in beginning a girls' ministry.

Prayer

Prayer is the basis for every aspect of ministry. The vision for girls' ministry must be God's and not yours. Remember, His thoughts are not your thoughts, and His ways are higher than yours (Isa. 55:8-9). Reading this book indicates that God is already at work and has put ministry to teenage girls on your heart.

- Seek His plan before you begin. If God is not in it, a ministry will not endure and flourish: "Many are the plans in a man's heart, but it is the Lord's purpose that prevails" (Prov. 19:21, NIV)
- Pray that God will show you whom He wants to coordinate this ministry in your church. You may be the coordinator, especially if God has put this ministry in your heart. If you are the student minister or pastor, pray for God's leadership in finding the woman to lead this ministry. Be open to leadership to come from unexpected places.
- Pray that God will touch the lives of teenage girls and open their hearts to be receptive and get involved.
- Pray that God will raise up women who will become mentors and be willing to share their lives with teenage girls.
- Pray for a purpose and mission statement so you can communicate the vision to others.
- Pray for the pastor to embrace this vision and be supportive of it.

Prayer is not only the beginning step, but it is also the foundation for the path that will maintain and grow this ministry. Involve others in praying. Be specific in the things for which you ask them to pray. Form a prayer team if your church does not already have one in place. Make sure you have God's permission before you proceed.

Share Your Vision with Church Staff

The input of your pastor and other church staff is vitally important before you begin a girls' ministry. The mission of girls' ministry should not only fit into the mission of youth ministry but also the mission of the entire church. The pastor and other staff members can give perspective you may not see. Pray together as a staff for this ministry. If you do not have the permission of your pastor, this may not be God's timing. Submit to the authority of your pastor, and watch God bless your existing ministry.

Choose a Leadership Team

If you are the staff member (pastor, youth minister, women's minister) in charge of ministry to teenage girls, choose a girls' ministry coordinator who will work under your supervision and authority. This woman should have a heart for ministering to teenage girls. Titus 2:3-5 gives the qualifications of a woman who is worthy to teach younger women. These qualifications will be discussed in detail later. You will not find someone who meets all of these qualifications perfectly, but if a woman is out of control in any of these areas, she will not be a good choice.

If you are a member of a small church, you may be the only woman who has a vision for girls' ministry, and you may only have a few teenage girls in your church. That's OK! Pour your life and energy into the girls God has put into your sphere of influence. Discipleship is best accomplished in small groups anyway. You may only have one group of girls. Start with what you have in your present situation.

If you are a member of a small church, you may be the only woman who has a vision for girls' ministry, and you may only have a few teenage girls in your church. That's OK! Pour your life and energy into the girls God has put into your sphere of influence.

If you plan a special event, invite other smaller churches or girls in the community to be involved with your church's event. In the past, I coordinated girls' ministry for churches in an entire county. Most of the churches had only a few girls. But when the girls got together for a girls-only conference, you would have thought they had been in church together all of their lives!

If you are in a larger church, form a team of godly women and diverse girls to study the needs of teenage girls in your community and church. The basic needs of girls are the same everywhere, but there will be specific needs based on the region in which you live, family situations, the social and economic status of families, and the culture of the area. This team can be a short-term team, or you may choose to use them on a long-term basis as an advisory team. You may need to meet with them on an intermittent basis or call them individually to get feedback and advice when needed.

Evaluate Current Programs, Ministries, and Events

Your current ministries, events, and programs may be meeting the needs of teenage girls adequately. Evaluate existing ministries. Do they simply need to be modified, or do you need to begin something entirely new? Get feedback from teenage girls, youth workers, parents, and other churches that are ministering to the specific needs of teenage girls. Survey the girls in your church to find out what their needs are and how you can effectively meet those needs.

Set Up a Mission Statement

Develop a mission statement and goals in line with the overall mission of your youth ministry and church mission statement. As you do this, focus on the specific needs of teenage girls. The girls' ministry team will work with the girls' ministry coordinator under the supervision of the pastor, student minister, or women's minister to set up the mission statement and decide how it will be accomplished. The girls' ministry mission statement for our church is "The Girls' Ministry of First Baptist Spartanburg exists to love and lead girls and their families into a personal relationship with Jesus Christ and to experience the joy of Christian fellowship with others; nurture them in their faith and affirm their gifts; and challenge and equip them to be disciples and become disciple makers that glorify God."

Here are some other sample mission statements and goals. While they are unique, they also share some similarities:

"Girls' Ministry at Whitesburg Baptist Church strives to testify to the gospel of God's grace by example and speech, to build unity, morals and self-esteem and to biblically ground teen girls of this generation." [1]

"The purpose of our girl's ministry is to reach out to every single girl (those who are lost, struggling, or growing). The girls are touched every week by someone who cares for them and loves them. Another purpose is to disciple girls. We want to show them that life is all about Jesus and for that to spill into every aspect of their lives." [2]

"The Quail Springs Church of Christ high school girls' ministry exists to help high school girls discover and grow into their role as godly women of character through the life-changing relationship of being God's daughter and belonging to a family of sisters in Christ." [3]

"In our high school group it is our desire for girls to come know God as the loving Father He is and to know that He has created each one of us with unique talents and gifts. We want to help girls learn what these talents and gifts may be and how they can use them to not only glorify God, but to also experience a satisfying life. Our deepest desire is for each girl to become a woman after God's own heart." [4]

Continually casting the vision for girls' ministry will help everyone stay on the same page and accomplish the purpose more effectively. Many times, the leader knows where he or she is going but forgets to inform others. When others involved in the ministry don't know the vision and direction, they often get lost in the shuffle. The leader can't understand why these volunteers are not doing their jobs. Many times, the volunteers simply don't understand where they are going and how to get there. It is the leader's responsibility to make sure everyone knows the destination and has the road map. Making sure each person involved has a copy or access to a copy of *Girls' Ministry Handbook* will be helpful in making sure everyone involved knows what they are trying to accomplish in the lives of teenage girls.

It is important to develop a leadership style that empowers those working with you to complete the task. Many times you will simply provide the resources for those actually carrying out the ministry. Working together as a leadership team is vital in the success of any ministry.

Recruit, Develop, and Train Leaders

Finding leaders and getting them to do their job adequately seems to be an age-old problem plaguing our churches. The keys to success in any ministry are recruiting and developing leaders, following-up and evaluating, and fine-tuning the ministry on a regular basis. This is especially true in working with teenagers. The principles of God's Word will never change; however, the methods we use to present the gospel must change regularly. This is especially true in youth culture because it changes at such a rapid pace. Recruiting and developing leaders will be discussed in greater detail in chapter five.

Communicate, Advertise, Publicize!

Publicity is important in attracting girls to your ministry. If their friends are involved, if it looks fun, and if it is relevant to their lives, teens will be more willing to give it a try. Personal invitations in the mail, e-mail newsletters, youth newsletters given out at youth events or meetings, and posters in strategic places frequented by teenage girls will communicate the beginning of your new ministry. However, girls personally inviting their friends is the very best method. Girls love to be with their friends. If they know their friends will be there, they will want to go! Recruit several girls with influence to invite their friends. Instant messages, e-mail, cell phones, and the Internet are important forms of communication for teens today. Most teens have e-mail addresses and instant messaging screen names. Build an e-mail list or instant messaging list and send an e-newsletter for your girls' ministry.

If your church has a Web site, designing a Web page devoted to this ministry is an important way to communicate with teenage girls. There is no one better to design a page for girls than another girl! Many teenage girls have good computer skills and are proficient in Web site construction. Use the girls in your church who have this skill to publicize the girls' ministry. Look at other sites that focus on teenage girls for the kind of look that will be attractive to girls. Most magazines that cater to teenage girls have Web sites and make it their business to know what attracts teenage girls. Get ideas from their site and use it to your advantage on your girls' ministry Web page.

Host a Kick-Off Event to Begin Girls' Ministry

An exciting kick-off event for your girls' ministry is an excellent way to generate interest in this new ministry focus. At this event, the vision for girls' ministry should be clearly communicated in an attractive way. The event should be fun as well as informative. Inviting mothers and your female youth workers will also create enthusiasm. Decorations should be attractive to teenage girls and the program should involve as many girls as possible. The women and teenage girls should feel ownership in the ministry. Involve as many women and girls in the planning as possible. Invite the youth minister or pastor to show his support for this ministry. Follow his leadership and communicate that he has the best interest of the teenage girls in your church at heart.

If you host a kick-off event, make to sure to follow through with developing the girls' ministry! A big event will create momentum, but if you let that momentum die, it will be hard to recreate the excitement.

Ideas for events such as banquets, girls' conferences, and retreats are outlined in the chapter on special events. If you host a kick-off event, make sure to follow through with developing the girls' ministry! A big event will create momentum, but if you let that momentum die, it will be hard to recreate the excitement. Having a plan in place for a continuing ministry will keep the energy, excitement, and enthusiasm going.

Evaluate and Make Necessary Changes

Evaluation of leadership and ministry to teenage girls is essential in successful girls' ministry. Ineffective programs or events waste precious time, energy, and money that could be used to reach girls for Christ and grow them into godly women. Plan events and ministry that have a purpose. Make sure every event, meeting, or small group falls in line with the mission statement that God gave you in the beginning. If it doesn't, then your church and your girls don't need to be involved in it.

Each of these steps to beginning a girls' ministry is vital in making the ministry successful, but prayer is the key. You can follow the steps perfectly, but the hearts and lives of teenage girls will not be touched unless God is present. You need His leadership and His wisdom. Your continual prayers will beckon Him to work. Pray and watch to see where God is working, then join Him in helping to raise a new generation of women.

Girls' Ministry in Larger Churches

If you are in a large church, the steps outlined in this chapter are crucial to the success and overall function of a girls' ministry. If you are the youth pastor in a large church, hiring a female as a part of your student ministry staff is one of the greatest things you can do! Probably half or more of the students in your ministry are female. Hiring a female to be a part of your team will lessen the load and enhance the ministry you already have in place.

What to Expect

Dr. Allen Jackson, youth ministry professor at New Orleans Baptist Theological Seminary, gave some valuable information on expectations between the student minister and the girls' minister at a girls' ministry class we co-taught at the seminary. Allen has given permission to use this material, taken from his class notes, for the purpose of this book.

If you are the student minister, these are the things you can expect from the girls' minister:

* **SUPPORT**— A girls' ministry should support the entire church program and student ministry. A girls' ministry should not compete or conflict with the church or student ministry.
* **COMMUNICATION**— A girls' minister should keep you informed about the girls' ministry plans, problems, and challenges. This may take place through planning sessions, staff meetings, or other times of coordination.
* **TEAMWORK**— A girls' minister or coordinator will not only be involved in girls' ministry programming, but also the total student ministry. If the youth group goes to a camp, retreat, or mission trip, she will be involved.
* **ADMINISTRATION**—A girls' minister should organize and implement girls' ministry events. She should also offer spiritual guidance for teenage girls, guidance for parents of teenage girls, and training and guidance for girls' ministry leadership.
* **INFORMATION AND EDUCATION**— The girls' minister can add a female perspective to the overall student ministry that can be invaluable. She can also be a source of information concerning female development, trends, and social issues.
* **RESPECT**— The girls' minister should demonstrate respect for you as the leader of the student ministry. She should also demonstrate respect to the rest of the church staff.

❋ A PROFESSIONAL, GODLY EXAMPLE—She should be careful how she interacts with you as the student minister, always guarding her purity and keeping her relationship with you professional and above reproach. You will have to be especially careful in not being alone together, traveling alone together, or developing an inappropriate relationship.

If you are the girls' minister, listed below are the things you can expect from the student minister:

❋ LEADERSHIP—The student minister is ultimately responsible for what happens in girls' ministry if it is under the umbrella of student ministry. You can expect guidance and protection from him or her.

❋ ORGANIZATION—The student minister should give you a job description and help you fulfill your responsibilities as the staff person in charge of the girls' ministry.

❋ RESOURCES—The student minister will provide the necessary resources for you to do your job with excellence.

❋ ACCESSIBILITY—You will need to be able to ask for advice and guidance from your student minister. It is wise to set up a time to meet on a regular basis, either weekly or at least monthly. Keep a running list of questions to ask in your meetings so you will not be continually asking questions every time you see him or her. This can be annoying to a busy student minister.

❋ TRAINING—Most student ministers provide intermittent training for their staff. The student minister may have funds built into the budget that will enable you to attend conferences each year to keep you fresh and up-to-date on youth culture and ministry to girls.

Beginning a girls' ministry in your church is exactly that...only the beginning. It will take several years to build a strong girls' ministry. Be consistent and don't give up! God is working all around you; are you willing to join Him in raising up a new generation of women?

Developing and Training Leadership

TRAINING WOMEN TO BE LEADERS in girls' ministry is foundational to the success of that ministry. You can organize a great kick-off event and draw interest from teenage girls, but if you do not have the leadership in place to carry out the ongoing work, a girls' ministry will not be successful. I often hear the cry from women, "I have a vision for girls' ministry, but I can't get anyone to help me!" or "I'm burned out because I am doing everything myself!" Smaller churches with only a few girls as well as larger churches with hundreds of girls need women who are willing to share their lives with teenage girls.

Where do you find leadership for your girls' ministry? What are the qualifications for leaders? How do you train women to lead girls? What do you teach them? These are legitimate questions that are key factors in a successful ministry.

I don't remember all of the Bible studies taught in my youth group, but I remember the example of my Sunday School teachers and Acteens leaders. I remember how they loved me and how they treated their husbands and children, as well as the funny things we did and the times we cried together when I had a broken heart. I remember the camps, retreats, and trips we took. I remember the times they rescued me when I was left out of the crowd and felt lonely. I remember some of the notes they sent when I was in the hospital at age 14. In fact, I still have them! I was looking through them recently and felt an overwhelming sense of thankfulness for the women who took time to love me as a teen.

One woman was especially significant in my life. Her name was Mrs. Lankford, and she was the director of Acteens at my church. She worked so many hours just to make our recognition services special when we had completed the steps in Acteens. I still have visions of her running around in the church sanctuary with her shoes off as she decorated the pulpit with white sheets and flowers. As I walked down the aisle in front of the whole church to receive my award for Scripture memory and missions work, I felt like a queen in the long white dress my mother had sewn. I remember how important it was to Mrs. Lankford that we complete those steps! At the time, I didn't understand why it was such a big deal to her, but now I do.

As I think about the qualifications for women who will work with teenage girls, I don't think about a woman who is perfect. I think about a woman who loves God and wants younger women to love Him, too.

Very seldom do girls thank me for working hard to make an event special. When I begin to feel a little weary and unappreciated, I think about Mrs. Lankford. Those memories spur me on to do my work with excellence. I know I forgot to thank her when I was a teenager, but in looking back, I deeply appreciate the time she spent teaching me how to be a godly woman. Most of the Scripture I know from memory is because Mrs. Lankford encouraged me throughout the memorization process.

She is elderly now and suffers from Alzheimer's disease. I saw her not long ago, walking at the mall with her daughter. I thanked her for the part she played in my life, but I don't think she recognized me. When I talked about the recognition services, though, I saw a sparkle in her eye that let me know those memories still linger deep in her soul. Mrs. Lankford wasn't perfect, but she loved God and wanted me to love Him, too.

Qualifications for Leaders in Girls' Ministry

As I think about the qualifications for women who will work with teen girls, I don't think about a woman who is perfect. I think about a woman who loves God and wants younger women to love Him, too. Titus 2:3-5 outlines characteristics for women who teach younger women. The Scripture lists qualifications of these women who will teach and behaviors for them to teach. Many times we don't consider teens to be younger women, but they are indeed women in training. Since girls learn from example, leaders should model in their everyday lives the characteristics they are trying to teach.

Titus 2:3-5 says, "In the same way, older women are to be reverent in behavior, not slanderers, not addicted to much wine. They are to teach what is good, so that they may encourage the young women to love their husbands and children, to be sensible, pure, good homemakers, and submissive to their husbands, so that God's message will not be slandered." Let's discuss these qualifications:

OLDER WOMEN SHOULD BE REVERENT IN THE WAY THEY LIVE—Showing respect or reverence is an important part of living a life of integrity. Respectful behavior to God and others is a necessary qualification of women in leadership. The word "reverent" in this passage is only used this one time in Scripture. It means "to conduct oneself in a manner appropriate for one who lives in the realm of the divine, walking in the presence of God."[1] Our lives are to "display a consecrated holiness to God"[2] in a manner worthy of our calling as God's beloved (Phil. 1:27).

Your life is a living video for younger women to view. In training youth leaders and parents, I often use the following illustration. I ask people to raise their hand in the air and make an "OK" sign. Then I ask them to bring their hand down and put it on their chin. I demonstrate the action while I speak, but I put my hand on my cheek instead of my chin. Almost every person will put their hand on their cheek instead of their chin. They feel silly when I ask, "Where is your chin?" The point is well made. Teens follow your actions, not your words!

Respect is like a boomerang. If you throw it out the right way, it usually comes back. When teens sense your respect for them they will respond to you in a more open way, and they will tend to offer you respect in return.

Respect is like a boomerang. If you throw it out the right way, it usually comes back.

WOMEN SHOULD NOT BE SLANDERERS—Other translations of the Bible use the phrase "not a malicious gossip." I've often wondered why this command was not in the list of qualifications for men. Evidently, God knows women have problems with slander and gossip. Words can give life or destroy it. Women in leadership must be good role models in the words they use. In discipleship and mentoring groups, the leader is responsible for the direction of the conversation.

If teenage girls begin to talk negatively about others, it is the responsibility of the mentor to stop the conversation in a kind and respectful way.

Prayer requests should be kept to the personal issues of those present, not the issues of those who are not there. Once the precedent is set and modeled by the adult, girls will follow suit. James 3:1-12 begins by saying, "Not many should become teachers, my brothers, knowing that we will receive a stricter judgment." This verse leads into a discussion about controlling the tongue. Verses 5-6 says, "So too, though the tongue is a small part of the body, it boasts great things. Consider how large a forest a small fire ignites. And the tongue is a fire. The tongue, a world of unrighteousness, is placed among the parts of our bodies; it pollutes the whole body, sets the course of life on fire, and is set on fire by hell."

When a person begins to tell you something about another person, and the Holy Spirit convicts you that it is gossip, it is OK to respectfully say, "I'm sorry, but I don't feel comfortable talking about this. Can we talk about something else, please?" Before long, your reputation will precede you, and people will not even attempt to gossip in your presence. It is a great feeling! Leading by example is important, but telling your girls you will not accept gossip within the group is equally as important.

Women who repeat information they have heard about others run the risk of communicating something that may be harmful or untrue. If you change one word in a sentence or even change your voice inflection or facial expression, you can change the meaning of the sentence. Try it! Choose a sentence and say the sentence over and over, emphasizing a different word every time you say it. Each time you emphasize a different word, the sentence takes on a different meaning. Whether written or spoken, words are powerful. Choose women to lead your girls' ministry who use their words to build up the kingdom of God.

WOMEN SHOULD NOT BE ADDICTED TO MUCH WINE—While this verse originally referred to older women who drank, the same principle of being controlled by something other than God's Spirit still applies. Women with personal addictions in their lives will not be good examples for teens. When addictions control a woman's life, it should be a red flag to herself and others. Self-control is a fruit of the Spirit and should be exercised in the lives of godly mentors. Alcohol, food, soap operas, shopping, tobacco, relationships, and many other activities control the lives of many women. Addictions begin in the mind. A woman thinks she must have the substance, activity, or person and then acts on it. Ask God to protect the minds and hearts of women in your church against believing the lies of the devil regarding addictions in their lives. Those addictions should be dealt with before a woman becomes a leader in girls' ministry.

WOMEN SHOULD TEACH WHAT IS GOOD—It seems this would go without saying, but many women model behaviors that are not good. The world bombards us with subtleties that are hard to recognize. When a woman is walking close to the Lord in her personal life and living in obedience to God's Word everyday, it is easy to teach what is good.

I had a conversation with a young woman I will call Susan who was in a mentoring program in her church. Susan's mentor left her husband simply because she no longer loved him. She continually criticized her husband in their mentoring sessions. When Susan informed the mentoring program's coordinator of the situation, she was reprimanded and told that she should try to be a good influence on her mentor and continue the relationship. What a tragedy! This coordinator did not recognize that this woman was not teaching what is good. Neither Susan nor her mentor benefited from this situation. When a woman is facing difficult situations that distract her from mentoring, or if she is not making good choices in her life, she should be asked to step aside from mentoring until she can get her life back in order. Women who mentor teenage girls should recognize truth, embrace it, and live it out in their lives.

Modeling is the best method of teaching the behaviors found in Titus 2. Therefore, these behaviors should be evident in women in leadership. These behaviors will be discussed at length in the chapter regarding small groups. The behaviors that a leader should model are as follows: she should love her husband and her children; she should be sensible in her actions; she should be an example of purity; she should take care of her home; she should be kind to others; she should be submissive to her own husband; and she should not dishonor God.

Because of our sinful nature, it is impossible to find a woman who measures up to each of these behaviors perfectly. Every woman may fail in one or more areas from time to time. The following is a good question to ask when seeking leaders for your girls' ministry: "Is this woman out of control in any of these areas in her personal life?" If so, she needs to be mentored by an older woman or counseled by a professional Christian counselor if necessary before stepping into a role of leadership for teenage girls. Girls are eager to mimic anyone who shows them love and attention. It would be a tragic mistake to give a woman a leadership role if she might lead girls in the wrong direction by her actions.

Potential leaders are all around you. Teenage girls need to be impacted and influenced by women of all ages and backgrounds.

One woman initially declined my invitation to work with teenage girls because she felt she did not know enough about the Bible to teach teens. This common misconception among women prevents them from experiencing the joy and blessing of pouring their lives into younger women. They seem to believe that a person has to be an expert in the Bible or a skilled Bible teacher to work with teenage girls. Nothing could be further from the truth. Love for God, a long list of good resources, a willing heart, a love for teen girls, and initial training followed by ongoing development will keep inexperienced mentors on the right track when working with teens. Women do need to be students of the Bible, however, in order to teach biblical principles to teens. Passing on what God is teaching you in your life is a great start in mentoring teen girls.

Where Do I Find Leaders?

Potential leaders are all around you. Girls need to be impacted and influenced by women of all ages and backgrounds. Working with teens has been given a negative slant, and women shy away from leadership responsibilities for many reasons. I once saw a cartoon of a pastor standing in the pulpit bribing nursery workers with a set of nice steak knives. The next caption read, "After the pastor's last recruiting effort, the nursery committee finally approved paid nursery workers." It is probably not a good idea to offer knives to leaders as a bribe, but you can't pay them either! The solution is to cast a paradigm shift that will help people understand that working with teenage girls is not a negative, grueling responsibility. It is one of the most rewarding and fun ministries in the church.

Bathe your efforts in prayer before you begin. As you start recruiting leaders, God will lead you to women whom He is calling to be involved in girls' ministry. Personally contacting women God has laid on your heart is the best method for finding leaders for girls' ministry. Training workshops for women who may be interested in working with teenage girls can also allow women to get an idea of what is expected from them and what the benefits would be. LifeWay offers training for women who feel God is leading them to be involved in girls' ministry. (Go online to *www.lifeway.com/women* for more information.)

Getting to know women in your church on a personal basis will enable you to see specific abilities that will be beneficial in girls' ministry. God does not gift every woman to teach Bible studies, but He does gift them in other areas of service. You may see a specific talent or gift in a woman's life. She may have the ability to organize, decorate, or communicate with girls in a special way. She may be fun-loving and creative. The more diverse the team you compile, the more well-rounded your leadership team will be.

There is a place of service for every woman in God's kingdom. Our responsibility is to seek God's direction in finding women whose place of service is in girls' ministry.

The size of your church does not matter. If there are fifty women or five thousand women, there are varying areas and degrees of ministry. Some women in the girls' ministry at my church decorate when we have an event and nothing more. Others mentor at risk girls. Some disciple and teach Bible studies every week. Others bake cookies or prepare meals, while some women help with stuffing envelopes and sending out invitations to special events. A group of women even set the tables with their own china when we had an etiquette luncheon for teenage girls! There are a couple of women who pray specifically for me and the girls' ministry. They are not involved in any other way. God will touch the hearts of those He calls to do a certain task. There is a place of service for every woman in God's kingdom. Our responsibility is to seek God's direction in finding women whose place of service is in girls' ministry.

Using Girls as Leaders

One of the greatest opportunities in girls' ministry is training girls to be leaders as they grow. Under the supervision of an adult, you can use high school girls as leaders with middle school girls. Utilizing college girls to be leaders with high school girls is beneficial as well. Younger girls look up to girls who are older than them but close in age. They connect in a way that can bridge the gap for girls and women.

I have worked with a specific girl for the past two years. Dani is an incredible young lady. She volunteers in the student ministry office and is very enthusiastic about calling other young people about events that are happening. Dani is an overcomer and an influencer! She was born with spina bifida but now has very few problems. She is a freshman in college now and studying to be a nurse. Recently, I received a call about a mother who has two teenagers. Her son, age 14, is autistic. He has seizures and needs constant care. Her daughter, age 13, never gets to come to church because she doesn't have transportation. I immediately thought of Dani. She drives right by the girl's house on the way to church. Dani was very excited to pick up this younger girl and bring her to church. She has even taken on a mentoring role in this girl's life.

Whether you are 25 or 55, you still need to build relationships with the students who are leaders and use them to influence other girls to get involved with girls' ministry. Girls want to know if their friends will be there. If they know the leaders are involved, they will sign up as well (most of the time). If they know the girl leaders think you are cool, then they will too.

Training the girls who are influencers and pouring your life into them will be a great benefit to your girls' ministry. Involving older girls in ministry with younger girls will help in growing them up to be godly women. Using college girls to lead workshops or Bible studies under your supervision is a great way to draw girls into the church. The very best way to train girls to be leaders is to allow them to watch you minister, to walk alongside you as you minister, and then give them opportunities to minister. You will be surprised at the potential teenage girls have when given responsibility with younger girls!

Legal Issues Regarding Leaders

Legal issues were not common in churches 25 years ago. In fact, it was unheard of for a church to be sued. Sadly, that is not the case today, and churches must deal with legal issues regarding the protection of minors. Sit down and talk personally with potential small group leaders or women who will have teaching responsibilities with girls, especially if you do not know them well. Many churches require volunteer leaders to fill out a leadership application and complete a consent form for a criminal background check. Questions about their previous experience with youth, personal testimony, volunteer experiences, former church memberships, spiritual gifts, and talents are vital in selecting volunteers. For women who have never worked with teenage girls or may be brand-new Christians, you may want to use them as an assistant to a more experienced woman for on-the-job training.

Providing a standard of reasonable care is important in protecting the lives of young people and the future of your church.

Many insurance companies today require churches to complete criminal background checks on all people involved with minors. It is vital to protect innocent teens from predators and the church from lawsuits. Most churches have a "six month rule" that prevents new people from serving with minors until they have been a member for six months, unless the person served successfully with minors in another church just prior to their move.

If a volunteer (male or female) abuses a girl in any way, the church and staff can be held liable. Most often when thinking about abuse, you typically think about males abusing teenage girls, but in today's society, that is not always the case. Sometimes women will get involved in a girls' ministry and develop inappropriate relationships with teenage girls, which can fall into the category of abuse. Performing a criminal background check may not prevent the abuse, but it will show your intent to protect teenage girls in your care. Many churches are sued and the doors are closed because the courts saw negligence on the part of the church's staff. Providing a standard of reasonable care is important in protecting the lives of young people and the future of your church.

Know the laws in your state regarding reporting abuse. In many states, church leaders are legally mandated to report abuse or suspicion of abuse within 24 hours of being made aware of the abuse. These laws vary in each state, but it will be worth your time to investigate and find out what your state requires.

Ongoing Leadership Development

Developing leaders is a never-ending task. There will never be a leader who knows everything because youth culture changes so rapidly. The gospel will never change, but the methods we use in meeting the needs of teenage girls must change continually. After women are trained in the basics of working with teenage girls, regular leadership meetings will continue to develop these women and keep their ministry fresh.

In smaller churches, there may only be one or two leaders for girls' ministry. Look for opportunities to learn from other churches, at the associational level, or through LifeWay conferences and forums. Take a couple of girls from your church and attend girls' ministries functions at larger churches to get ideas. Come back to your church and decide how you can use those ideas to fit the needs in your church.

What Should Be Taught?

Preliminary training sessions for girls' ministry should involve the information presented in this manual. In addition, the following information will be beneficial to leaders.

* **GIRLS' MINISTRY VISION**—The vision of girls' ministry, communicated clearly on a regular basis, will enable leadership to stay focused and to work together for a common goal. When women in leadership get off track and begin to plan too many activities, the vision or mission statement will draw them back into perspective. Develop a mission statement and bring it before your leaders often. If you are the only leader, then read it often, especially when planning events or planning to teach. Everything you do as a girls' ministry needs to support that mission statement.

* **SPIRITUAL GIFTS ANALYSIS**—Leaders will benefit from learning what spiritual gifts the Holy Spirit has given them and how those gifts can be used to serve. Every Christian woman has one or more spiritual gifts, but many do not realize they have a gift or know how to use it. Spiritual gifts assessments are helpful in getting women in the right position as a leader. You might consider leading volunteers through the study *Jesus on Leadership: Developing Servant Leaders* by C. Gene Wilkes.

* **PERSONALITY TYPES**—Leaders will benefit from learning their personality types and how to teach girls according to their personalities. Responding to girls according to their personality types will enhance relationships between women and teenage girls. PLACE Ministries provides resources to help Christians find their place of ministry within

the church. PLACE is a five session assessment and study that teaches about personality, spiritual gifts, abilities, passion, and past experiences. It then discusses how God uses all of these areas to help every person find their place of ministry within the body of Christ.

* **LEADING SMALL GROUPS**—Each discipleship leader should be trained in leading small groups and have effective communication skills. Learning methods to control excessive talking and keep the girls on track is important. Knowing when to put the book aside for a teachable moment is key as well. Getting every girl involved in the discussion and not allowing one or two girls to dominate is another valuable skill for leading small groups.

* **TEACHING METHODS**—Leaders should be trained in using curriculum and teaching methods. Students learn differently. Some are visual learners, while others are reflective, musical, or verbal learners. A good leader knows to utilize different methods in helping students discover truths in God's Word.

* **YOUTH CULTURE**—Leaders should keep up-to-date in the rapidly changing youth culture. Media literacy is important in reaching and teaching teens today. Different Web sites are listed on the resource pages to help you in keeping up-to-date on youth culture and media related to teenage girls.

* **POLICIES AND GUIDELINES**—Because church guidelines change annually, it is important that these be communicated verbally and in writing if possible.

* **OVERALL CHURCH GROWTH**—Leaders should be a part of the overall church program and taught the basic church doctrines.

Ongoing leadership training is necessary for follow-up, evaluation, and fine-tuning your girls' ministry. At least once a year, training and leadership development will enhance even the best leaders. LifeWay offers leadership training for girls' ministry, and many Baptist seminaries see the need and offer seminars and even master's degree programs related to girls' ministry.

CHAPTER 6

Small Group Discipleship & Mentoring

BUILDING RELATIONSHIPS should be a high priority in working with teen girls. A teenage girl will receive the truth more easily from a woman with whom she has developed a strong relationship. In looking back over ministry through the years, I have noticed one common thread: when women took the time to develop close relationships with the girls in their groups, the girls were more likely to stick with discipleship until they graduated.

How do you develop a relationship with a teenage girl who has absolutely nothing in common with you? By spending time together, talking about hurts and joys, laughing, crying, praying, letting your guards down, acting silly, and studying God's Word together, you will often find that she is simply you, many years ago. Mentoring and discipleship groups afford the opportunity to build relationships with teenage girls who desperately need women who love God to show them how to love God, too.

The Definition of Mentoring & Discipleship

There are many definitions for mentoring and discipleship, but we will define these terms in relation to girls' ministry: *mentoring* can be defined as coming alongside a young woman to model godly womanhood, teach biblical truths, and train her through life's experiences. *Discipleship* can be defined as leading and training a young woman to be a follower of Jesus Christ. Mentoring and discipleship go together like a car and tires. One does not fulfill its purpose without the other. Basing your mentoring and discipleship on God's Word will help you mold and shape teenage girls into the likeness of Christ. If a teenage girl is mentored but not taught biblical principles and truths in God's Word, she will not fulfill her God-given purpose. In this book, the term *small groups* will be used to describe the setting for both mentoring and discipleship.

Small Groups Are Best

Individual mentoring works well for adult women, but mentoring teenage girls one-on-one is not a good idea. Rare situations with exceptional women and teens will be appropriate for one-on-one mentoring, but as a general rule, mentoring or discipleship groups are best. There are several reasons:

1. THE BASIC RELATIONSHIP NEEDS OF GIRLS ARE MET—When a girl is involved in weekly discipleship and held accountable for her quiet time, her relationship with God will grow. Weekly mentoring and discipleship with one or more adult women will enhance her need for relationships with significant adults. When small groups of girls meet weekly to study God's Word, pray for one another, talk through their problems, and just have fun, their need for healthy peer relationships is met.

2. SMALL GROUPS ARE WISE BECAUSE OF LEGAL ISSUES—Churches are being sued at a steadily increasing rate in the U.S., and many of the cases involve minors. Small groups provide protection for the girls and the adults.

One woman learned the value of mentoring groups and having at least two leaders in the group. During one group meeting, she was leading the girls to discover how they can overcome temptation in their lives. She made the comment, "When you girls make wrong choices and give in to temptation, I take that as a personal failure." A couple of girls in the group who had been involved in partying were not there that night to hear what this leader said. Some of the girls present told those girls that their leader had talked about them behind their backs and had said their partying was a bad reflection on her. Those girls were devastated to think that their discipleship leader would discuss their behavior with the other girls in the group. Of course, their leader was innocent, but the rumor seemed real. The only thing that saved that leader's reputation was the fact that she had two other adults in the group to verify her innocence. While this was not something for which the leader could be sued, it certainly could have destroyed the girls' trust in the leader.

Not only can trust be destroyed, but many serious legal issues may arise as well. Church leaders and volunteers are only one accusation away from ruin. The accusation does not have to be true—the mere possibility of wrongdoing can be enough to destroy a person's character, reputation, and ministry. Meeting with girls in small groups provides accountability for the girls and the adults involved. If a private conversation needs to happen, make sure you are meeting in a semi-private place to talk. A restaurant or an area of a room where other people are in view will work for this kind of situation. Women should never meet alone in their home or the girl's home. Lives and reputations have been ruined because of an unhealthy emotional or physical attachment.

Lives and reputations have been ruined because of an unhealthy emotional or physical attachment.

Many girls are emotionally unstable because of their home situations, abuse, or neglect. This emotional struggle is made worse by our culture, which fosters deviant sexual identities among teens today. Magazines, TV programs, movies, and books encourage teenage girls in lesbian feelings and behavior. Because of rape, molestation, and incest, many girls have an intense hatred for men. When nurtured by another female, the teen may mistake their care for romantic love. Women who work with teen girls must be aware of this potential pitfall. Relationships with girls must be kept in the proper realm for protection of the girl and the adult. Boundaries must be set and never crossed.

3. SMALL GROUPS ARE MORE COMFORTABLE—Some girls believe that adults do not really like them and don't want to be with them. They feel strange sitting down alone with an adult. The small group setting alleviates that uncomfortable feeling of not really knowing what to say. Plus, girls feel more comfortable with their peers present. They often feed off of other girls' comments. Some girls may not feel comfortable voicing a problem, but if another girl voices a similar struggle, everyone in the room benefits from the mentor's godly counsel based on biblical truth.

Structure and Organization

Setting up small groups will vary from church to church. Groups are usually more effective when two women meet with four to ten girls. Each woman should have no less than two and no more than five girls to mentor. More or less can be overwhelming or uncomfortable.

Your group can meet whenever it is convenient for the women and girls. If you have enough girls in your church to form more than one small group, the youth minister or person in charge should set the guidelines for each group. Some groups meet early in the morning before school. Some meet on Sunday nights. Others meet during the week. If you have a large youth group with several small groups, it is usually better to pick a specific day and time for all groups to meet. While the meeting places may vary, organization and accountability for group leaders is easier when groups meet on the same day and time.

Meeting places may vary from restaurants, homes, church classrooms, or other places, like a teen center or coffee shop. Restaurants offer more distractions unless you are able to find one with a private meeting room. In larger cities, it is often more feasible to meet at the church because of travel distance and time. However, meeting in your home is the ideal setting because it provides a comfortable, relaxed atmosphere where girls will see you in action with your home and family.

Responsibilities of the Mentor

Women who want to mentor teen girls must be willing to accept the responsibilities involved. Listed below are a few tasks related to mentoring girls:

❇ COUNT THE COST OF INVESTING IN GIRLS' LIVES. In today's society, teen girls experience very few stable relationships. One day the girl may have a family, and the next day, mom or dad has left. Boyfriends come and go, often leaving a broken heart in their wake. Girl politics leave girls wondering which friends they can really trust and which ones might stab them in the back. Many girls cannot bear another disappointment or, in their eyes, another rejection. "Our adolescent girls aren't looking for tourists—adults who are only interested in seeing the beautiful spots, taking a few quick pictures, and then leaving after a week to go back to their comfortable lives at home. Rather, these girls are looking for pilgrims... who aren't looking for the comfortable, easy path but are willing to take the hard road of understanding the issues that adolescent girls face, issues that are unprecedented in their magnitude."[1] Counting the cost before deciding to mentor will prevent the disappointment of a failed mentoring relationship because it was not well thought-out from the beginning. The following questions will help you make this decision:

1. Do you have the time to spend each week with teenage girls?
2. Will this commitment leave time for your own family?
3. Are you willing to love the girls unconditionally through good times and bad?
4. Do you need to give up other commitments in order to mentor girls?

❋ **MEET AT LEAST ONCE A WEEK IN SMALL GROUPS.** It is usually best to use a discipleship curriculum to ensure accountability in the topics being taught. Most people need a guide from which to teach. The staff person responsible for small groups should assist in choosing biblical, solid, practical curriculum. A list of resources for girls' ministry and mentoring are in the back of this book.

❋ **KEEP IN TOUCH WITH YOUR GIRLS DURING THE WEEK.** Make phone calls, write notes, and send e-mails, IMs, and text messages. Dropping by a sporting event or special occasion will also foster a deeper relationship.

❋ **PRAY FOR THE GIRLS ON A DAILY BASIS.** Ask for prayer requests each week. Sticky notes and index cards are wonderful tools on which the girls can write their prayer requests. These should be kept in a convenient place so you can pray for the girls often. Make sure they are not left where others can see confidential information. You will learn a great deal about the girls you are mentoring through their prayer requests. Small prayer notebooks are also a good idea for each girl to keep. They can write down each other's requests and pray for each other throughout the week. Girls love seeing someone at school from their mentoring group and being reminded that they were prayed for that morning!

❋ **ENCOURAGE DEPENDENCE ON GOD BY HOLDING GIRLS ACCOUNTABLE FOR THEIR DAILY QUIET TIME.** Initially, this may involve teaching girls how to have a quiet time. There are many devotional books available for teens. LifeWay publishes *ec* (*essential connection*), a daily devotional magazine for teens. You may order these through your local church. You will also find a quiet time guide printed at the end of this chapter.

❁ **Hold Girls Accountable for Other Areas of Their Lives.** Teen girls need accountability in their relationship with Jesus, their relationships with others (friends, family, boys), and their emotions. The following questions are guidelines in holding girls accountable in these areas:

1. What did you learn from God's Word this week?
2. How did you guard your heart and emotions this week?
3. Did you chase boys this week? What steps will you take to change this behavior?
4. How did you develop your godly character this week?
5. Did you lie about any of the above?

❁ **Keep a Sense of Humor in Working with the Girls.** Mentoring teenage girls is serious business, but you must maintain a balance between teaching and fun. Let your hair down so they can see you act crazy at the appropriate times. Sleepovers or other fun activities are a great time to be silly and enjoy being with each other. Sometimes girls are shocked to know their leaders are real people! I remember one occasion during a Christmas party, we had a video scavenger hunt. We had to do all kinds of crazy things and make a video. We were racing to beat all of the other teams back to the church. I have never laughed so much in all my life. After that, all the girls came back to my house and spent the night. So many girls slept on my floor that I ended up sleeping under the Christmas tree. The girls couldn't believe I didn't sleep in my bed, but I didn't want to miss any of the fun. We made breakfast the next morning and lounged around until noon talking and laughing. To see me without make-up, my hair sticking up, and brownies in my teeth was just about more than they could stand!

Responsibilities of the Girls

While the leader of a small group bears a great responsibility in mentoring teen girls, the girls need to decide if they want to make the commitment to be involved in a small group. Leading a girl to decide if she can make this commitment is important. Helping her to count the cost before she commits to a small group will prevent problems after the mentoring relationship begins. Mentoring relationships require willingness from both parties. When beginning a mentoring program in your church, some parents will try to coerce their daughters to be involved. They have good intentions and want the best for their daughters, but if the teens are not willing, it can be a difficult situation. Some churches have created a commitment form or card for each girl to read and sign. This commitment is a safety net for girls and their leaders. It is a form of accountability and gives the leader the right to approach, in love, a girl who is gossiping, not having her quiet time, etc. Faithful attendance and keeping up with the discipleship assignments are equally important. This commitment card is a tool for accountability. The following is included on most forms or cards:

1. I COMMIT TO ATTEND ALL SMALL GROUP MEETINGS FAITHFULLY. Most girls need accountability to keep their priorities in order. If a girl commits to the group but only attends once a month, it breaks the unity of the group. Each week the girls experience spiritual and emotional growth. When a girl misses several weeks, she misses out on those opportunities for her growth. When a girl is absent and not growing in her relationships (with God, adult mentor, or peers), it disrupts the purpose of the group.

2. I COMMIT TO COMPLETE ALL DISCIPLESHIP ASSIGNMENTS FAITHFULLY. Completing the work is a discipline that will help girls grow spiritually. When girls are held accountable for studying God's Word, they will begin to grow. God's Word applies to every aspect of a teenage girl's life. As they spend time with God, they will begin to realize this and develop a hunger for His Word.

3. I COMMIT TO KEEP CONFIDENTIAL ALL PERSONAL INFORMATION SHARED IN THE SMALL GROUP. I UNDERSTAND THAT IT IS THE LEGAL RESPONSIBILITY OF THE ADULT TO REPORT TO THE APPROPRIATE PERSON ANY INFORMATION SHARED REGARDING ABUSE OR HARMFUL BEHAVIORS. This is a safety net for the girls' very lives! Often a girl will share something in a small group they have never told anyone else. They are more inclined to share deep feelings in a group of this sort. They need to know they can feel safe in sharing their deepest thoughts. The girls need to understand they must not share what is talked about inside the group with people outside the group. This provides a safe place for each girl to share her feelings without thinking she is going to hear it at school the next week.

The adult must abide by this rule as well. It is easy for women to tell others about a personal prayer request she hears. This is unacceptable in a small group setting. Praying to God about the situation is the only avenue that is acceptable unless the girl or someone else is in danger. If a girl shares that she is being abused in any kind of way, it is the responsibility of the adult to report this to the appropriate authority. Most states mandate reporting abuse or even suspicion of abuse. The staff at your church will know the protocol for reporting such information.

When discussing this guideline with the girls, it is important to explain that you will not gossip about their problems. However, if something is going on in their lives that is harmful, you do promise to tell only the person who needs to know. They must trust you to do the right thing with this information.

If the girl is involved in illegal or harmful behavior such as an eating disorder, cutting, drugs, or alcohol, it is important to tell the student minister or pastor. He will follow the protocol of the church and inform the appropriate person. Ask him if there is anything else you need to do, and then it is out of your hands. You will continue to minister to the girl as you did before. She may be in the hands of a professional counselor, but you will continue to mentor and disciple her if she is willing.

4. I Commit to Keep Myself Pure in Thought, Word, and Action.
Accountability for a girl's actions is important during the teenage years. Peer pressure is one of the biggest problems girls face. They need someone to ask them hard questions about their actions. Ask each girl to write on an index card those things for which she needs to be held accountable. Keep the cards and ask each girl questions regarding her individual needs in this area.

5. I Commit to Pray Faithfully for Other Members of This Group.
Praying for one another on a regular basis draws the girls closer together. Some girls even develop a signal to use at school that says, "I'm praying for you today!" You can learn a tremendous amount about the girls in your group by listening to their prayer requests. I know of one leader who kept a prayer journal for each girl and gave them her prayers for them when they graduated from high school and left the group for college. Some girls choose to keep a prayer journal themselves in which they write down prayer requests each

week. It is important to warn girls to not leave their prayer notebook unattended in a public place since the prayer requests of others are private and confidential. It is a good idea to write very personal requests in codes.

6. **I Commit to Develop My Relationship with Jesus Christ by Having a Regular Quiet Time, Praying, and Attending Church.** Modeling and teaching girls to pray, study their Bible, and be accountable for attending church is an important part of discipleship. Teenage girls need to know that prayer is not simply a wish list. Through an intimate prayer life with God, He will change their lives and the lives of people for whom they pray. God's Word is applicable to their lives, and fellowship and corporate worship are vital in their lives as Christian young women. When they are held accountable for being involved in the overall church program as they grow, they will be more likely to continue this involvement when they leave for college. A growing relationship with Jesus Christ is the goal of discipleship. This commitment is the foundation for the Christian life.

Helping girls work through the common everyday problems of a teenager's life is part of mentoring, but counseling for more serious problems is unwise. If you are not a professionally trained counselor, this is a very dangerous situation.

Counseling vs. Mentoring

We see many problems in the lives of today's teenage girls—problems more complicated, more distressing, and more overwhelming than ever before. For this reason, it is very easy for an adult to slip into a counselor role instead of maintaining a mentoring role. Helping girls work through the common everyday problems of a teenager's life is part of mentoring, but counseling for more serious problems is unwise. If you are not a professionally trained counselor, this is a very dangerous situation. Wrong advice may endanger the life of the teen or another person. One well-meaning pastor counseled a teenager who was contemplating suicide. The teen seemed to feel better as he left the pastor's office, so the pastor did not inform the parents or get professional help for the teen. Later that night, the teen wrote a suicide note mentioning the pastor's name and killed himself.

Knowing when to refer a girl to a professional counselor is important. Your youth minister or pastor is a good resource. When you run into problems that are out of your league, call your student minister or pastor for advice. Always keep your youth pastor informed when serious problems occur with the girls in your group. Most church staff, especially youth ministers, will have Christian counseling resources to refer teenagers to when necessary. Several books related to teen issues andcounseling are listed in the back of this book.

Confidentiality is another important issue when working with teens. The following statement is common from teenage girls to the women who mentor them: "I want tell you something, but you must promise not to tell anyone." This statement should send up a red flag immediately. This is a promise you cannot keep, legally or morally. You will be wise to promptly answer: "I can't make that promise, but I can promise that in the event I do need to tell someone for your protection, I will only tell the person or persons who need to know. You have trusted me this far; please continue to trust me to do the right thing to get the help you need." When training women who work with girls, confidentiality is an important issue to discuss. It is unethical and inappropriate to discuss confidential matters with friends, family, or other youth workers.

In the event the safety of the girl or someone else is at stake, you should only tell those who need to know. It is a good idea to develop a church-wide policy and train people working with children and teens on the reporting methods and practices. Most states have laws pertaining to reporting abuse, intent to harm oneself, and/or intent to harm another person. Most states offer "good faith reporting" allowing one to report these situations anonymously. In certain situations, it is the legal responsibility of clergy to report to the department of social services or the police in your area when the safety of a minor is at risk. As church leaders, it is wise to learn the laws of your state. Your church's attorney, an attorney who attends your church, or the local department of social services should have information regarding those guidelines. Your church needs to develop a procedures policy so all leaders will know the church's process in reporting abuse. Having a plan already in place ensures the safety and well-being of everyone.

Who Should Not Mentor Teenage Girls?

We discussed the qualifications of women who should be leaders for teenage girls, so let's discuss who should *not* be mentors for teenage girls. The Bible clearly states that older women should teach younger women and older men should teach younger men. It seems this paragraph would not be necessary, but unfortunately, my experience is to the contrary. Throughout my years of ministry, I have often seen male youth ministers or male youth workers who thought nothing of developing a close relationship with a teenage girl. Maybe this girl did not have a good family life, and the youth minister intended to give the girl a relationship that was missing in her life. In every one of those situations, someone got hurt. A male youth minister can be a spiritual influence in the life of a teenage girl, but when they develop a close intimate relationship, it may be hard for either of them to keep their thoughts and actions pure.

A prudent youth minister will not be involved in close mentoring relationships with teenage girls, nor will he allow male youth workers to do so.

When thinking of the guidelines God has set forth in His Word, we always see His guiding hand of protection. The same holds true in this situation. This principle shows God's protection for the girl and for the man as well. God knows us better than we know ourselves. Not only are legal issues involved, but there are moral and emotional issues at stake as well. Emotionally deprived young girls are not able to handle a close mentoring relationship with a male. Many young girls' hearts have been broken when they fell in love with a youth minister or a male youth worker who tried to mentor them. There is no such thing as an innocent crush. Young girls are always hurt when a crush is allowed or encouraged. This can be the thing that gets her off track in her relationship with God.

We also see the hand of protection for the youth minister or male youth worker. Many men are not strong enough spiritually or physically to control themselves in a mentoring relationship with a young girl. An innocent, young girl is easily defrauded in a close mentoring relationship with a male. Many girls are attracted to any male who shows them the slightest bit of attention. Whether a man is innocent in the area of a sexual relationship with the girl or not, he is responsible for his actions in defrauding her emotionally. First Thessalonians 4:3-6 warns against sexual immorality and defrauding others in this area. In ministry, one careless act can ruin a life and ministry. The results of a relationship taken too far are devastating for everyone involved.

A prudent youth minister will not be involved in close mentoring relationships with teenage girls, nor will he allow male youth workers to do so. There is a need for godly men in the lives of teenage girls but within proper boundaries. A wise student minister will continually make sure that women are being trained to mentor teenage girls on an ongoing basis. Mentoring and discipleship groups may be set up as co-ed groups with a husband and wife team leading them. When it comes to accountability time and actual mentoring, the group can split to focus on gender-specific needs.

What Should I Teach Teenage Girls?

Titus 2 is very specific in the behaviors that we, as older, more mature women, should model and teach to teenage girls. Modeling and teaching these principles will not only honor God, but it will result in saved lives, less emotional and spiritual bondage, and fewer problems in their futures. They will grow up to be women who know how to love God and be obedient to Him in their daily lives. Let's explore further what older women should teach teen girls.

To Love Their Husbands

Hopefully, the teenagers you mentor will not have husbands, but they may soon. A little girl first learns how to be a wife by watching her mother's example. Unfortunately, many teen girls today do not have a positive, loving example. It is not uncommon for a teen girl to see her mother abuse or be abused by her husband, be involved in serial monogamous relationships with other men (or other women), or even be sexually promiscuous. To counter this negative influence, you can be an example by loving your husband. Teaching girls how to relate to the opposite gender in the appropriate way is foundational in their relationships with their husbands in the future. Even if you are single, you can model purity, modesty, and respect in your dating relationships.

Respectful and honorable relationships with the opposite sex in the teen years will foster the same kind of relationships when girls grow up and get married. Teaching a girl to set biblical dating standards is an important aspect of preparing her to love her husband in the future. Guide her in deciding what she will and will not do on dates. Setting standards before she is in a compromising situation is important because the decision is already made. By setting standards, writing them down, and reviewing them often, she will keep her goal in mind. A person without standards never lives up to anything. If she makes bad dating choices, she may end up with many regrets in her marriage. Every date is a possible mate. Prevention ministry in this area is priceless.

Respectful and honorable relationships with the opposite sex in the teen years will foster the same kind of relationships when girls grow up and get married.

Teaching a girl what godly characteristics to look for in a young man is also important. One of the most frequently asked questions is, "Should I date non-Christians?" We need to challenge young women to follow biblical instruction in every aspect of their lives, including the guys they choose to date, knowing that God's instructions are for their benefit, not to limit their freedom or choices. Teaching a girl to make wise choices in dating will enable her to truly love her husband in the future.

To Love Their Children

Most teenagers you mentor won't have children, but unfortunately, some might. Pre-teen pregnancy is happening more often because girls physically mature earlier and are not being taught to strive for purity in their lives. If the girls you mentor have children, you can mentor them on the job. If the girls you mentor do not have children, teach them how to love their future children.

How do you teach someone to love? First, you must model love to them. Then they must see you model that love to your children. The following ways are examples of loving children:

1. PROVIDE FOR THEIR NEEDS—It is important to help girls understand that they can actually provide for the needs of their future children even before they are ever born. You can teach girls that abusing drugs and alcohol now may affect their children in the future. Such abuse may cause birth defects, addictions, and so on. Growing spiritually now will prepare her to provide spiritual nurturing for her children in the future. Preparing herself intellectually by get-

ting a good education will better equip her to teach and train her children. An uneducated parent will not have the experiential background to know how to provide intellectually for her child as well as an educated parent. The bottom line is that an emotionally stable, physically healthy, spiritually mature mother can focus more on her children and love them more effectively. That foundation begins in the pre-teen and teen years. (If the teen already has a child, explain that using drugs and smoking in the presence of the child are harmful to the child's health.)

2. BEGIN WITH A LOVING HOME—An older woman can teach a young woman to prepare for a loving home now by helping her make good choices in the young men she dates. Guide her in setting standards for dating. Give her accountability in keeping her standards. Guide her to decide what kind of man she wants to be married to for the rest of her life. Encourage her to write down those characteristics and measure every young man she dates by those standards. Lead her to understand that she cannot change a young man's character after they are married. Just because he lets her put a wedding ring on his hand does not mean he will begin to be a faithful mate or calm his raging temper. A strong, loving, healthy marriage is a critical foundation for bringing children into the home.

Getting rid of immature ways in your life and modeling mature behavior is part of mentoring teens to love their future husbands and children.

3. GET RID OF CHILDISH WAYS IN YOUR LIFE—If you have ever been around teenage girls for very long, you will notice that they often exhibit childish ways in their relationships with others. They pout, tattle, cry, pitch temper tantrums, and say mean things to others. We see movies about mean girls, read books about them, and hear a lot of feedback from teen girls about the mean girls they know. Teaching girls how to get rid of childish ways in their lives will not only help them have better relationships as they grow older, but it will also result in mature women who will be ready to model good behavior for their children.

First Corinthians 13 is well known as "the love chapter" and has the answer to getting rid of childish ways. The whole chapter focuses on love, except one verse, or so it seems. Verse 10 focuses on childish ways and putting those behind as a person grows into adulthood. Why is this verse in the love chapter? What are childish ways?

As a general rule, children display selfish behaviors. Pouting, crying, yelling, throwing temper tantrums, running away, tattling, hitting, whining, threatening, refusing to talk, and throwing things are only a few of the tactics children use to get their way. Hopefully, as the child grows more mature, the childish ways will slowly diminish. But unless the child has a good role model to teach and train them, the childish ways will spill over into their adult life. Many adults live with childish behaviors controlling their lives. They pout, cry, and yell to get their way. Their displays of anger, bouts of not speaking to one another, and threatening looks and actions rule their families. Getting in the car and squealing the tires after an argument or walking out and refusing to discuss an issue in a sensible way are equivalent to taking your toys and going home. As children, they may have learned these actions from significant adults in their lives. When they grow up, they model these actions for their children, thus continuing the cycle of generational sin. God's message in 1 Corinthians teaches us to get rid of childish ways. Why? Childish ways destroy relationships between husband and wife, parent and child, or in a family, a church, or between friends.

You can help teenage girls to break the generational cycle of childish ways that will destroy love relationships in her family.

Getting rid of immature ways in your life and modeling mature behavior is an important part of mentoring teens to love their future husbands and children. Once a teenage girl learns this principle of God's Word, she can begin to work on one childish way at a time. When she has matured in one area, she can move on to the next. By eliminating these harmful ways in her life as she grows, she can be ready to model maturity and love to her children. By holding girls accountable to change those immature ways, you can help them break the generational cycle of childish ways that will destroy love relationships in her future family.

To Be Sensible

Teaching teenage girls to make wise choices based on God's Word will result in sensible behavior. It involves teaching girls how to think critically by walking them through decisions they face. Mentors must teach them how to deal with situations by turning to God's Word and relying on the wisdom He provides.

Always telling a child what to do and not to do prevents them from learning how to think through situations and make wise decisions for themselves. If children grow up with an adult always making decisions for them, they will succumb easily to others who tell them what to do. You can guide a teenager in making wise decisions by asking questions that will help them learn to think through the factors, variables, and consequences. A friend relayed a story to me about a girl who confided in her about cheating. The adult mentor simply asked the girl what her choices were (to cheat more, to study, to confess to her parents that she'd cheated and now needed a tutor to catch up). Once the girl listed the choices, they talked about the consequences of each. After weighing each one, the girl made her decision. While this was a minor issue, these small decision-making situations can help prepare girls to face larger ones.

Mentors must teach girls how to deal with situations by turning to God's Word and by relying on the wisdom He provides.

Teaching girls to depend on the Lord—instead of you—for answers will help them make sensible decisions in life when you are not there. For example, you may be mentoring a girl who is emotionally needy. She may call you often with problems. You give her biblical answers and try to teach her truth. If she would follow your advice, you know her problems would be less dramatic, but she refuses. She may call you again and again with the same problems. By the time you finish the conversation, you are exhausted mentally and physically. You are frustrated and feel in your heart she just wants the attention you give her, not an answer to her problem. She becomes totally dependent on you. You begin to feel burned out and find yourself avoiding her.

Teaching a girl to depend on the Lord takes only a few simple changes in your approach. It may take a while for her to get used to the new method, but she will soon begin to get the picture. When she comes to you with a problem that is addressed in Scripture, provide her with that Scripture. Tell her to go to a quiet place. This could be a table in the corner of a Sunday School room, a pew in the sanctuary of your church, or in her room at home. Tell her to sit down with her Bible, pen, and paper. Instruct her to read the Scripture, tell God her problem, and ask Him to show her what His Word says about the problem. Instruct her to write what comes into her mind. The most important step is for her to come back and tell you what God said to her. Sometimes a girl may struggle with making God's Word apply to her particular situation, so you might need to walk her through the passage to help her see how it relates.

83

It is vitally important for you to check what she has written to make sure she is on track. If she has written something that does not line up with God's Word, show her the contradiction in the Bible, ask questions, and guide her to the correct answer. Through this exercise, she will learn to go to God's Word, think through her decisions, and pray for God to show her the answers. You will not always be there to give her the answers in life. Teaching girls to go to the Lord and His Word is a valuable tool in teaching them to be sensible.

To Be Pure

Purity involves the entire person—mind, body, and heart. People tend to think of purity in a physical context, but sexual impurity stems from the mind. Teaching girls the truth of God's Word will help them to think, speak, and live a life of purity—in their dating relationships, the movies they watch, the things they read, the Web sites they visit, and the speech they use.

A study in the American Journal of Sociology revealed that teenagers who pledge to remain sexually abstinent until marriage are 34 percent less likely to have sex than those who do not take virginity vows. This study also reports that the biggest factor to having sex is being in a romantic relationship, but teens who are in relationships and take abstinence pledges are less likely to have sexual relations than teens who don't make a pledge.[2] A commitment to purity along with accountability is an important factor in helping girls remain pure. Teaching teen girls to focus on friendships instead of romance is also important. However, we are missing the boat if we teach abstinence without an emphasis on total purity—purity of the mind and heart as well as the body.

Living out a life of purity is the best way to teach girls how to remain pure. A story is told of a World War II Nazi concentration camp in which men and women died of starvation daily. The end of the war came, and American soldiers parachuted into the camp to take over and let the prisoners know that help was on the way. As one soldier was going through the camp reassuring those who had been so brutally abused that everything would be okay, he came into the living quarters of an old woman. The woman's body was caked with dirt. It must have been months since she had been able to even wash her face and hands. Her clothing was threadbare and filthy, and the stench of her living conditions was sickening. The smile on her face told the soldier that she still had hope in her heart. As the soldier turned to walk away, the woman offered him a portion of the bread that had been air-dropped into the camp. The soldier saw the woman's hands cradling the bread. The thought of eating it made him nauseous, and he kindly refused. There was nothing wrong with the bread; he just could not accept it from the woman's dirty hands. Here's the parallel: there is nothing wrong with the Bread of Life, but many people have a hard time accepting it from impure hands. Our lives must mirror what we challenge girls to live.

To Be Good Homemakers

In today's culture, Paul might have been considered oppressive or chauvinistic in stating that younger women should be taught to be "good homemakers" (Titus 2:5). However, an understanding of the culture in which Paul wrote would prove otherwise. In the first century, the home was the place of central influence for a woman. Paul was simply addressing women where they were, empowering them in their major sphere of influence at the time. He understood that:

> "Whether a woman works outside the home or not, she is to bring special graces and beauty to her home. More than any other member of the family, the woman tends to set the tone for the household. Paul is commending women who understand the importance and high priority which God has designed into the roles of mother, wife, and homemaker. Society rests not on politics and commerce, but more critically upon the home..."[3]

It is important for teen girls to understand the unique role they will play in the family they will have in the future. Even if some remain single, the home can be a place of mercy, hospitality, grace, and hope to others. And whether or not a girl chooses to marry, she still needs to be taught basic household skills like cooking, as these are skills that are often lacking in this generation of micro-

---

waves and take-out. Teaching teenage girls how to cook and perform different tasks around the house are wonderful mentoring activities. Inviting the girls you mentor into your home and modeling a godly household can be a tremendous example to them. When doing mission projects, allow the girls to cook, make crafts, or do household tasks for the elderly. Through your example and their hands-on experience, they will learn how to make their homes a place of delight when they grow up and have households of their own.

One small group adopted an elderly lady in our church. The girls thought they would bring her cookies and sing to her as she sat in her rocking chair, but they were in for a shock! She invited the girls into her home for a Thanksgiving meal. She taught them how to cook the meal, set the table, and even instructed them on table manners. She told them stories about her younger days and life lessons she had learned through the years. This was the beginning of a long relationship. Not only did this lady now have a reason to get up in the mornings, but the girls learned how to be workers at home as well.

God does not view women as tagalongs, second-thoughts, subservient, or secondary. They are critical, crucial, with a vibrant role to play.

To Be Submissive to Their Husbands

The world teaches women—even teenage girls—that they should not submit to men, period. This is partly true. God's Word admonishes wives to submit to their husbands, not to all men in general without discrimination. I think this misconception needs to be clarified for girls, and they need to realize the specifics. When singled out, the concept of submission makes women bristle (no one likes to be controlled), but when taught in the context of God's plan for the family, it is easier to accept. God's plan is not only for a woman to submit to her own husband, but for a husband to love and care for his wife like Jesus loved the church! He loved the church and gave Himself up for it, and He submitted to God the Father in order to take care of the church. What woman wouldn't want a husband who loves her enough to give his own life and submits to God in order to protect her? It is our responsibility to teach teenage girls this biblical truth at a young age before their beliefs are formed otherwise. Why? The Bible is very clear in the answer: that the Word of God may not be dishonored.

The best way to teach this truth is to model this action in our daily lives by being subject to our husbands in attitude, word, and behavior. God created males and females equally but with different roles within the family. These roles provide a picture of who God is and how He relates to His people. Jesus is equal to God but yet submissive and responsive to Him. God loves His Son and exalts Him. Adam was created first and given the responsibility to provide, protect, and lead. God saw it was not good for man to be alone, so He made a "helper who is like him" (Gen. 2:18). *Helper* is not a subordinate term. In fact, the word doesn't really describe heart of the meaning of the Hebrew words from which it was translated, *ezer kenegdo*.

> "The word *ezer* is only used twenty other places in the entire Old Testament. And in every other instance the person being described is God himself, when you really need him to come through for you desperately... Most of the concepts are life and death, by the way, and God is your only hope. Your *ezer*. If he is not there beside you...you are dead. A better translation therefore of *ezer* would be 'lifesaver.' *Kenegdo* means alongside, or opposite to a counterpart. " [4]

Does this help you understand the irreplaceable role that wives play in the lives of their husbands? God does not view women as tagalongs, second-thoughts, subservient, or secondary. They are critical, crucial, with a vibrant role to play. Teen girls need to understand and embrace this role.

Results of Mentoring

How do you measure the success of mentoring? If the girls are able to recite their memory verses each week, does that equal success? If they fill in the blanks in their discipleship books, are you triumphant? When a girl admits she has not had her quiet time in three weeks, does this mean the mentoring group is not working? The answer to all of these questions is no.

Girls' ministry discipleship and mentoring is a process, not a program. This process will go on even after the girls graduate from high school and go on to college. You may see indicators along the way that your efforts are encouraging the girl on to maturity, but it is difficult to measure success in mentoring a girl. When you see maturity in a girl's life and she begins to reach out to others and mentor them as well, that is a strong indicator that you have been successful. The girl may reach out to a friend and guide her through a rough situation by communicating the truth of God's Word and then working through the process of making a wise decision with her. When the girl being discipled becomes the discipler, then you will know you have been successful. You must be patient to see that happen, and you may not see the results until many years later.

Mentor and Mobilize

In one of my first mentoring groups, I started with two girls. We met at the church for 10 weeks. They had a hunger for the Word of God and were like sponges. At the end of 10 weeks, I asked them to choose a friend to be involved for the next 10 weeks. Those four girls became my mentoring group for that school year. The next school year, I asked each of those four girls to choose a younger teenage girl and invite her to join the group. We began meeting in my home and covered the same material again. This time the core group gave testimonies and taught the lessons under my supervision. When it came time for accountability, we separated into groups of two in different areas of my home. The older girls asked the accountability questions and prayed with the younger girl they were mentoring. When it was time for the younger girls to leave, I met with the original four for accountability and planning. Those girls are now out of college today. One is the director of preschool and children's ministry in a church. Another is an attorney practicing law that protects the religious and civil liberties of Americans. The third is a missionary in Eastern Europe. The fourth works in a children's hospital and has grown into a remarkable young woman. All of these young women today are mentoring younger women.

When you model godly principles, mentor girls, and give them an avenue of practicing what they have learned, the natural phenomenon of multiplication will take place. When teen girls begin to grow in their relationship with the Lord and see what He can do in their lives, they will tell their friends. When you promote peer evangelism and mentoring in your group, the girls will begin to catch the vision for mentoring their friends. Sowing mentoring seeds in a young girl's life will reap a great harvest. Commission your girls to become campus missionaries. Help them develop a strategy for sharing Christ.

The school campus is the largest gathering of teenagers and the biggest mission field for this age group. Unfortunately, teachers and school administrators can be terminated for sharing their faith on the school campus. In some areas of the country, youth pastors and youth workers are not allowed on the school campus for the purpose of evangelizing. In the area where I live, youth ministers and mentors are allowed on campus only to build relationships with students, not to evangelize.

However, the Equal Access Act[5] and the Students' Bill of Rights allow teens to witness by forming Christian clubs as long as they do not interfere with teaching. Today's teens have an opportunity to take the gospel of Jesus to this great mission field, more so than any generation in the past. When girls are spiritually transformed and mobilized, they can become peer evangelists and lifestyle mentors. How might this take place?

Lifestyle Mentoring

In most classes, a student can reach out and physically touch eight fellow students: one on each side, one in front and back, and four diagonally. Challenge your girls to perform random acts of kindness each day for those eight students. They may loan a pen or piece of paper. They may give a compliment. They may offer to help with a difficult assignment. Once they have befriended that person, it will become easier to talk about what God is doing in their lives. Teach them how to give a two-minute testimony of what Jesus Christ has done in their lives. (Simply tell what your life was like before Christ, how you realized you needed Him, how you became a believer, and how your life is different because of Christ.) Most students are in four to seven classes per day. Each girl has the potential to reach up to 56 students per semester. They may not be able to mentor that many students one-on-one, but they can be an influence.

Encourage the girls to have their spiritual antennae up, always looking for girls to mentor. By teaching them how to give a two-minute testimony of what Jesus has done in their lives and encouraging them to reach out to friends in need, you can instill the vision of peer mentoring in the girls. Let them know you are available if they face a situation they cannot handle. Teach them how to recognize a situation they cannot handle and instruct them in steps to take.

When you pour your life into girls and they continue the process, the number of girls being discipled doubles continually. Soon you will see the process of multiplication in action. Teen girls can play a tremendous role in completing the Great Commission.

Quiet Time Guide

1. Choose a time, and make an appointment with God. Choose the same time every day if possible. This will keep you disciplined.

2. Choose a place. The place should be quiet, with few distractions. Choose a favorite spot outside if the weather permits. Or choose a quiet place in your room or other place in your home.

3. Bring your Bible, a pen, a journal, and a devotional guide. Choose a Bible translation that is easy for you to understand. There are many devotional guides from which to choose: *ec* (Essential Connection) and *DevoZine* are two good ones. Christian bookstores also carry devotion books.

4. Begin with prayer. Ask God to speak to you and help you understand what you read. The Bible is God's love letter to you.

5. Read your devotional and then read the Scripture indicated.

6. Write down the important points in the Scripture and how God is speaking to you about what you have read.

7. Close with prayer. Talk to God just like you would talk to a friend. (He is your Friend!) You may like to write your prayers to God. When God answers a specific prayer, go back and check it off with a red pen. This will help you see how many times God answers your prayers.

It may be difficult at first, but before long you will begin to look forward to the time alone with God. God will speak to your heart about lots of things— like relationships, obedience, and decisions in your life. God is more interested in your heart than what you do for Him, and He wants to change your heart. You will begin to notice a difference in your attitudes and actions. God loves you so much. He wants to spend time with you everyday!

CHAPTER 7

Special Events
for Teenage Girls

AT DIFFERENT INTERVALS during the year, it is important to bring teenage girls together for special events geared toward their unique needs. Girls-only retreats or conferences, mother/daughter events, father/daughter events, and sleepovers are all big hits with preteen and teenage girls. Mentoring activities and mission trips are also vital to teaching young girls to be godly women as well. Special events for teenage girls can be fun, and they offer another opportunity to help young women become more mature spiritually, physically, mentally, emotionally, and relationally.

Can you imagine having a makeover conference for guys, showing them how to apply makeup properly, sift through the latest fashions to find modest alternatives, manicure their nails, understand the male mind, and become a godly young woman? Neither can I, but these are important issues for teenage girls!

In the book, *Captivating: Unveiling the Mystery of a Woman's Soul,* John and Stasi Eldredge wrote, "We think you will find that every woman in her heart of hearts longs for three things: to be romanced, to play an irreplaceable role in a great adventure, and to unveil beauty. That's what makes a woman come alive."[1] Some girls have been hurt and have hidden deep in their souls the desires that God has placed within them as young women. We can plan special events to emphasize the things girls know about and identify with to bring them to the truth that the King desires their beauty (Ps. 45:11). They need to know that He has a great adventure planned for their lives, and they have an irreplaceable role to play. We can plan events to show girls that He loves them beyond comprehension (Eph. 3:18-19) and has written a love letter (Scripture) just for them!

Smaller Church/Larger Church Events

If you are from a smaller church, don't skip over this chapter! There are plenty of ideas here geared toward smaller churches as well as larger churches. Two things to keep in mind: first, when planning special events for teenage girls, smaller churches can gather with other churches in the area as sponsors. Second, large churches can publicize and invite smaller churches to be involved in the special events at their church. Joining forces allows churches to impact girls on a larger scale.

I heard a story once about a little girl in a small rural town. One day she wandered away from home and was missing for several hours. The town folk came together and began searching for her. They tried to cover as much territory as possible, but darkness set in, forcing them to abandon their search. The next morning, the people of the town met and prepared to go out again to search for the girl. One of the men had the idea for everyone to form a straight line and join hands. As they searched every inch of the area, they found the little girl's body. The girl's mother cried out, "If we had just joined hands sooner, my little girl would still be alive!"

The lives of teen girls are at stake. Let's join hands and work together before it's too late. Girls' ministry can become the catalyst that draws us together to work for His kingdom plan.

Planning Purposeful Special Events

Special events should be planned with a specific purpose, and that purpose should always fall in line with your mission statement. This does not mean you cannot have an event purely for the purpose of getting girls together for fellowship. Fellowship is vital in the relational area of a girl's life! If your mission statement includes enriching the lives of teenage girls spiritually, mentally, emotionally, physically, and relationally, then the options are endless. Some important thoughts on planning special events for teenage girls are as follows:

❋ Consider retreats, conferences, sleepovers, mother/daughter or father/daughter events, shopping trips, etiquette luncheons, fashion shows, makeover workshops, girls' nights out, and weekly or monthly guided "girl talks" geared toward specific topics of interest for teenage girls in your church. Even if you are in a small church, these events (sleepovers, shopping trips, and "girl talks" will work with two to three girls and a couple of moms or leaders. Homes are wonderful sites for these activities. For conferences, fashion shows, and other larger events, gathering with other churches will make it more feasible financially and more enjoyable for the girls.

❁ Choose and plan these events with respect to the entire youth ministry calendar and for a specific purpose. Be aware of the church and youth ministry calendar. If you are in a small church, don't allow small numbers to be an excuse for poor planning. Plan events for small groups the same as you would plan for a large group—with excellence. Get out the real china for that etiquette luncheon. Show the girls that they are important even if there are only two or three girls. They will be surprised and feel special if you go the extra mile just for them.

❁ Your church budget also will determine the number of special events you will be able to plan during the year. Many events can be done with little cost to the church or the participant, but they should always have a purpose. Using women in your church to lead breakout sessions will save money on speakers. Finding a group of college students who have a band will save money on music for the event. Find a mother who enjoys cooking to organize the food. Maybe once a year, your church budget will allow an outside speaker, a band, or catered food. Depending on your individual church, a nominal fee to cover the costs of the event is appropriate, keeping in mind that some girls might not be able to pay. This gives people who have been blessed financially the opportunity to provide a scholarship for girls who can't pay.

❁ More than likely, many women in your church would love to share their talents with teenage girls. When starting the girls' ministry at our church, we announced the "girl talks" and asked women to let us know what talents they possessed that could be used to teach teenage girls. We had women who wanted to teach etiquette, basic modeling, writing, scrapbooking, personality training, dating standards, nutrition and exercise, and much more. A gynecologist in our church wanted to share her expertise in the areas of sexual purity, coping with adolescent issues, and abstinence with preteen girls and their mothers. Another woman wanted to bake cookies for the girls to enjoy at their events. The women in our church were so excited to know God could use their talents and that teenage girls wanted to learn from them. These topics were things that teen girls were interested in and knew about, so we used them to draw out spiritual truths in their lives. Jesus did the same thing when He used fish, sheep, water, and bread to draw spiritual truths in the lives of people. When teaching a workshop with girls, think about ways to connect the topic with a spiritual truth. Suggestions are given in the "Ideas for Special Events" section.

Questions to Ask When Planning

WHY SHOULD WE DO THIS EVENT?—When planning a special event, the first question to ask is, "Why should we do this event? What do we want to accomplish with the girls?" You must then decide what kind of event would best accomplish your goal. For example, if you want to foster relationships between mothers and their daughters, would you have a mother/daughter retreat, conference, shopping trip, or banquet? This decision will be based on several factors—the youth ministry and church calendar, your budget, and the girls and mothers in your church. What event would they respond to best? Would they respond to an event at the church or an overnight trip? Are the families in your church able to pay for an overnight retreat, or do you need to have a potluck banquet at the church?

WHEN IS THE BEST TIME FOR THIS EVENT?—Another important question to ask is, "When is the best time to host this event?" Coordinating with the church calendar, the youth ministry calendar, school events, and community events will help determine the potential attendance at the event. I once planned a community-wide girls' conference and forgot to check the school calendar. It was a small town, and the high school had a very large band. The state band competition was the same day of the girls' event. Not only did the band members and their parents attend the competition, but many others in the town showed their support as well. Needless to say, attendance at the girls' event was low.

WHERE SHOULD THIS EVENT TAKE PLACE? —Where you have the event will play a large part in determining its success. One church planned an overnight conference for teenage girls. They wanted to have the event at a nice hotel, but did not consider their budget. The girls had elegant rooms in an upscale hotel, but there was not enough money to provide adequate food during the conference. The girls spent most of the weekend being hungry. Some girls even pooled their money and ordered a pizza in the middle of the night! On the other hand, a girls' conference held at the church allowing the girls to decorate classrooms like a girls' bedroom would have been more effective. The girls' focus would have been on the important things instead of their tummies!

Smaller churches have an advantage because homes are a wonderful place to host special events. With a small number of girls, you can plan a special event in someone's home. Sleepovers, mother/daughter events, father/daughter events, and even makeovers can all be done in smaller, more intimate settings. Homes provide a wonderful atmosphere in which to build relationships. Even guided "girl talk" is a great way to mentor girls in a home setting. On the other hand, many retreat centers and conference centers are cost effective if girls want to get away.

WHO IS THE TARGET AUDIENCE?—The next question to ask is, "Who is the target audience for this event?" Is it an outreach event where you invite girls from the community and other churches? Is the event designed to promote unity and growth for the girls in your own church family? Is your target group middle school, high school, college, or all of these groups? Do you want to involve moms, dads, or just the girls?

In larger churches, groups may be divided into age groups simply for logistics, but in smaller churches, groups may meet together. When meeting together, it is important to consider age-appropriate topics and activities within the group. Younger girls simply do not have the cognitive capacity to think in abstract terms like older girls can. And sometimes younger girls lack the emotional maturity to tackle deeper issues connected with sexuality, relationships, and other related topics. In smaller churches, this may be an obstacle you face.

In planning events for teenage girls, adequate adult supervision and volunteers are vital to the success of the event. One girls' ministry coordinator planned a large event for mothers and daughters in her church. She tried to do everything on her own and refused help from many women in the church. The event turned out to be a disaster. She was on stage trying to emcee the event even though she was a very shy and serious lady. She prayed, played the guitar, and led the praise and worship music. She did ask someone else to speak but failed to communicate a time limit. By the end of the evening, the girls and moms kept restlessly looking at their watches. She failed to ask participants to make reservations and had over one hundred more people than she planned. She ran out of food, tables, and emotional energy. By the end of the event, she had learned a great lesson, but it cost her the position as girls' ministry coordinator at her church. A sample worksheet for organizing a planning team is included in the event planning guide at the end of this chapter. Involve as many people as you can in the event. Learn to delegate, follow-up, and cover all of your bases. If you are not a detailed planner, enlist someone with that talent to help you.

WHAT WILL THE PROGRAMMING BE?—The program is a key part of the event. Choosing the right speaker, musician(s), small group leaders, topics, breakout sessions, ice breakers, skits, video clips, and testimonies will help accomplish your goals for the event. Keeping your target group in mind will determine what kind of music you have, the age and focus of the speaker, and so on. The music will set the mood of the large group sessions at a conference. Music can be used to motivate girls, help them have fun, and at the right time, bring them into the presence of the Lord for worship. Keep a file of speakers and musicians who would be appropriate for your group of girls. Women in your church may also be good resources. Don't choose someone just because she is your friend. Make sure you have prayed about this person and that she is the right one for the event.

HOW WILL PUBLICITY AND REGISTRATION BE HANDLED?—You can plan an incredible event, but if the girls don't know about it, they won't come. Sounds silly, doesn't it, to plan an event and not publicize it? You would be surprised how often this happens. A simple announcement in the church bulletin on Sunday will not catch the attention of teenage girls.

Thinking of an idea on Monday and trying to pull off the event on Saturday is difficult unless you only have three or four girls in your youth group. Even in a small church, you may find yourself alone on Saturday! Planning ahead and building momentum for the event will boost the number of girls who will attend. Determining if the event is for outreach or to build group unity will also determine where and how you advertise. One church planned a girls' event, purchased a huge banner, and hung it at the busiest intersection in town. Churches from all over the city brought girls to the event simply because they knew about it. Advertising in the newspaper, on the radio, and through Christian clubs at schools are also good ways to let others know about your event. But the very best way to get girls to come is a personal invitation from friends. Choose key girl leaders who are respected and ask them to commit to the event and spread the word. Girls want to know if their friends are going, and the first question they usually ask is, "Who is going to be there?"

Asking girls to register and pay beforehand is a good way to know how many girls to expect in attendance. Setting a deadline for registration is also a good idea. Asking girls to register is a wise use of church money; if you plan an event and spend money on it, but the girls do not show up, you have used God's money unwisely. Selling non-refundable tickets for an event is a sure way to cover your expenses and boost attendance.

WHAT IS THE BUDGET?—Wise use of your church's money is vital. Setting a budget ahead of time and sticking to it as much as possible will show integrity on your part. In the special event planning guide at the end of this chapter, you will find a budget planning guide to assist you. Determining how much money you have budgeted, the number of participants you expect to attend, and how much you will charge each participant will depend on the target audience, location, and program.

Follow-up

Many times after an event is over, the coordinator is ready to move on to the next project. However, follow-up and evaluation are crucial to the success of future events. The planning team should sit down together and discuss the successes and the inadequacies of the event. If you are in a small church, follow-up may be easier, but it is still important. You may be the only person involved, but it is still important to sit down and ask yourself what you can do better next time. An evaluation sheet may be given to the girls at the end of the event for comments and suggestions. These suggestions can be hurtful if you take them personally and view them as criticism. Do not allow one negative comment among lots of positive ones to ruin your enthusiasm for ministry. When you receive a negative comment, ask yourself: "Is this comment true? If so, what can we do to improve the next event?"

Thank-you notes to the planning team, speakers, musicians, and anyone involved in the event are fundamental to promote service in the future. Also be sure to write your pastor a note thanking him for his support and encouragement. If other women helped you, write them a note even if you are good friends! People need and want to be sincerely thanked. A simple comment, phone call, or e-mail is better than nothing, but a note received in the mail is a priceless treasure to many who have given their personal time to serve with you.

Following up on decisions that girls made during the event is necessary to continue growth in their lives. Girls who accepted Jesus Christ as their personal Savior or recommitted their lives to Him may need more counseling. They also need to speak with your pastor about baptism or other public displays of their commitment. Pray sincerely for requests girls voiced. The girls need to receive confirmation that you or someone else is praying for their needs, so be sure to send a note or e-mail.

It's in God's Hands, Not Yours

The mark of a good coordinator is never losing your cool, even when things don't go the way you planned. Sometimes God tests our dependence and trust in Him by altering our plans. I planned a mother/daughter conference one weekend at our church. I invited an all-girl singing group from Tennessee. That weekend, a huge ice storm was forecasted to hit our city. When I heard the weather forecast, I started a phone tree, calling all the participants and instructing them to bring sleeping bags and extra clothes. The storm held off until midnight on Friday. The girls and their moms slept in the church, and we had a wonderful conference despite the inclement weather. The singing group was snowbound in Tennessee and never made it to the conference. At the last minute, I invited four well-liked guys from the youth group to come and impersonate the singing group. They wore mops on their heads, makeup, dresses, and high heels. (They went home immediately after their debut before the ice storm hit!) We used a CD for our praise and worship music. The girls loved it, and the weekend turned out to be a great spiritual awakening for those involved. Prayer, preparation, and planning are vital for the event, but remember that God is ultimately in control. All the preparation in the world will be futile if God does not show up at your event. Your prayers and the prayers of others will beckon Him to be there.

Ideas for Special Events

SHOPPING TRIP—If you plan a shopping trip, the purpose may be to guide girls in choosing clothing that is attractive and modest, not seductive. Pairing a younger girl with a cool college girl or young adult woman to shop for attractive clothing will be a great mentoring activity. You may take the event one step further as a competition to see who can come up with the most attractive outfit for the least amount of money. Having a fashion show afterwards to model the clothing—complete with judges—could add excitement to the event.

In my church, we planned an overnight trip with mothers and daughters to go to a large mall in Atlanta and then stopped at an outlet mall on the way home. It was a fun day for the mothers and daughters. We planned it around the holiday season, so it was a great time to do Christmas shopping.

FATHER/DAUGHTER CELEBRATION—Teenage girls love to dress up and look pretty, and they love to spend time with their fathers. Our church capitalized on these two facts by celebrating the relationships between fathers and daughters. We hosted a dinner in the fellowship hall of our church. One of the mothers decorated the stage, tables, and an area to take father/daughter pictures. A father/daughter team spoke and another sang the special music. We gave every father and daughter a three-week devotion booklet written especially for them to do together. We chose different daughters, fathers, and mothers to write the devotions for each day and titled the booklet "21 Days To Your Daddy's/Daughter's Heart." To cap off the evening, each father read a covenant of purity to his daughter promising to live in a way that would protect his daughter's heart and purity and then signed it for her to keep as a personal treasure. The event was a home-run!

When you plan an event such as this, you must prepare for the likelihood that some girls will not have fathers to attend the banquet. If this happens, ask godly men in your church to step in for the evening. Choose these men carefully and make sure they are of the highest character. Have these men meet their "adopted daughters" at the church. This will guard against any discomfort and preserve decorum.

POWDER-PUFF FOOTBALL—Many girls love to play sports of various kinds, but they will rarely join in with the guys to play. Two years ago, I asked our pastor's daughter what kind of special event she would like to have for the girls. She immediately replied, "Powder-puff football!" I set out to plan a powder-puff game for the girls. We had so many girls sign up that we needed four teams! Not only did the girls from our church sign up, but girls from the community also called to register. We decided to make this an outreach event and advertised in the community. Each girl paid $20 to play. This covered her lunch, powder-puff T-shirt, and insurance for the game and practices. We had four men from our church coach the girls. The first year we hosted this event, the boys dressed as cheerleaders, but the next year they became the assistant coaches. Both worked well. We scheduled practices on two Sunday afternoons prior to the big game. The coaches not only taught the girls how to play flag football, but they emphasized godly character and sportsmanship, keeping the most coveted award in mind: Most Christlike Player. We had the game on a Sunday afternoon. All four teams played, then we had a winner's play-off game and a loser's play-off game. Every girl played two games. During halftime we had a fifteen-minute devotion and presented the plan of salvation. One father accepted Christ!

Parents and students who were not playing came to watch and brought blankets, picnics, and lounge chairs. We hang a plaque each year in the student center honoring the winning team. This has become an annual event in our girls' ministry and is one of the favorite events of girls, parents, and even the guys!

Just a side note about dividing teams fairly: the coaches met and divided the teams. Then after the teams were divided evenly, they picked their team out of a hat. The goal is not so much winning as it is fellowship, character building, and evangelism.

Even if you are in a smaller church, a powder-puff football game can still be a great event. Make it a game between two churches or even groups of churches. This could be the very thing that draws folks in your community together!

 (CHICK CHAT—Chick Chat is guided small-group discussion for teenage girls. We allow the girls to write down topics of interest, and they meet on Wednesday afternoon before our youth worship time. The topic is decided ahead of time, along with questions and Scripture. College girls and young adult women who are godly role models lead the large group time. The girls then meet in groups of two or three with another college girl guiding the discussion. They look up Scriptures pertaining to the topic and answer life questions based on the Word of God. This is a relaxed, fun time, and the girls benefit as well. This is especially interesting to middle school girls.

If you are in a small church, this can easily be done. You might need to meet as one larger group or in two or three smaller groups, depending on your size. Ask godly women in your church to help with teaching and breakout groups.

GIRLS' ONLY CONFERENCE—A girls' only conference is a one day conference with a speaker, music that girls love, and breakout sessions that pertain to the interests and needs of teenage girls. It can be done at your church and will involve ladies from your church. Ideas for breakout sessions are:

- Dealing with Daddy (Learning to understand your earthly father and how that reflects on your view of your heavenly Father)
- When God's Girl Prays (The potential of a girl's prayers)
- What Do Guys Really Think? (Panel with two to three godly young men whom girls respect)
- Dating (Setting standards and looking back with no regrets)
- Exercise and Nutrition: God's Plan for a Healthy, Beautiful You!
- Personality 411 (Learning to get along with everyone)
- Express Yourself: Learning to Decorate your Bedroom
- Mean Girls (How to deal with them and not become one yourself)
- Miraculous Manicures (Keeping your hands beautiful, not only the way they look, but the things they do! Do you use your hands to do kind things, love others, and encourage others? You can have perfect nails but if you use your hands to hurt others, they are not really beautiful.)
- Makeup Makeovers (Cosmetologists and makeup consultants are always happy to help with this workshop. Beauty is not merely skin deep! Inward beauty is emphasized in the large group sessions.)
- How to Decorate Your Dorm Room (Tips for going away to college)

ETIQUETTE LUNCHEON AND FASHION SHOW—This can be a part of a girls' only conference, but it can also be a stand alone event as well. If you are in a smaller church, you can easily have an etiquette luncheon in your home. It is important to use real china and have the table set correctly. If you choose to do this in your church, ladies may volunteer to bring their personal china and decorate each table with a different theme and china pattern. Recruit someone to lead the girls through table manners as they eat their meals. (Etiquette books are easily found in the library, and any woman could brush up on her table manners to lead this session.) The girls love it, and everyone has a good laugh or two during the meal. If you decide to include a fashion show, it is a good idea to use girls in your church as the models. Make sure you preview the clothes the girls choose before they come out to model. Sometimes their opinion of appropriate clothing leaves something to be desired. You always want to promote modesty, but at the same time you want to show the girls how to dress attractively. Some department stores are willing to do fashion shows as a way of promoting business.

BIBLE STUDIES—Girls'-only Bible studies provide a place for girls to open up God's Word without the distractions of what the guys are thinking and doing. Girls are more free to ask questions, share openly, and offer insights if they are in a safe environment among other girls. The studies can focus on issues specific to the needs of teen girls. In addition, Bible studies that focus on women of the Bible teach girls that God has a plan for their lives. The resource section contains a list of Bible studies geared specifically for teen girls.

GIRLS' MINISTRY KICK-OFF EVENT—Planning an event to promote the beginning of a girls' ministry in your church is a great way to build momentum and get the word out about the ministry. You may want to invite moms to be involved as well. Make sure you include food, fun skits, music, and a presentation of what girls' ministry will look like in your church. You may want to invite a special speaker to challenge and encourage the girls to be involved. Make sure you have a leader or leaders in place to continue the ministry after the kick-off. If you wait too long, you will lose momentum, and the girls will lose interest.

PRAYER AND PAMPERING—Our church does a mission trip to Kentucky every year where we conduct Vacation Bible School. The teens work very hard and are often frustrated and tired when they arrive back at the college where we sleep. In the afternoon, the adult ladies on the trip have a Prayer and Pampering session for the girls. We set up a room with lotion, praise and worship music, manicure supplies, and chocolates—a must! We ask the girls to wash their feet before they come, and the ladies massage the girls' feet with lotion and paint their toenails if the girls want. While we are kneeling before them massaging their feet, we ask for specific prayer requests for their ministry. This is great relationship-building time. The girls are humbled to see their leaders kneeling to massage their feet and pray for them. The guys want to get in on this one, but—sorry guys!—this is a girls-only event.

MOTHER/DAUGHTER EVENTS—Events involving mothers and daughters are crucial in building a girls' ministry in your church. These events can range from mother/daughter banquets to mother/daughter sleepovers, or even a mother/daughter tea. Knowing the mothers and daughters in your church will determine the kind of event you plan. Getting feedback and help from the moms and daughters will be essential in the planning. If you plan an event from your ideas only, they may not show up, but if they help to plan the event, they are sure to be there.

In churches where there are many damaged relationships between mothers and daughters, it may take a little more patience and effort, but it will be worth it in the end when you begin to see those relationships grow. Often daughters do not want their moms involved in anything they do. When digging into these relationships you will often find that the mother may be critical and outspoken where her daughter is concerned. Working with mothers and modeling for them how to treat their daughters may be necessary before the daughters will agree to be with their moms in front of their friends. Start with the moms and daughters who are willing to attend and then build from there.

These are only a few of the special events for teenage girls that can be planned in your church. Girls' ministry must be intertwined with the overall youth ministry. Check to see what events are already planned and piggy-back on those events to minister to girls. Prayer and Pampering is a good example of a piggy-back event. Be creative! Keep a list of special events that you do and share them with others. Everyone needs fresh ideas from time to time.

Special Event Planning Guide

Planning Team

The event coordinator will work with all of the other coordinators to make sure plans are being made and carried out on time. This team will make sure everything is being done. The number of people available in your church determines the number of coordinators involved. Each coordinator is not solely responsible for their area but will recruit the people necessary for that team's success.

1. Event Coordinator: _____

    (Oversees event, coordinators, and will possibly be in charge of the program.)

2. Prayer Coordinator: _____

    (Organizes prayer for the event, speakers, musicians, and prayer requests before, during, and after the event. Contacts girls after the event letting them know someone is praying for their requests. This position is key to an event's success!)

3. Programming Coordinator: _____

    (Secures speaker and musicians, sets schedule, determines theme, and works with financial coordinator and event coordinator to stay within budget.)

4. Hospitality Coordinator: _____

    (Coordinates greeters, food, giveaways, packets, pictures, and decision counselors. Works with financial coordinator to stay within budget.)

5. Publicity Coordinator: _____

    (Coordinates all publicity, media, mail-outs, and flyers. Works with financial coordinator to stay within budget)

6. Financial Coordinator: _____

    (Works with church staff in setting budget, and works with each team to stay within their budget. Takes care of money for registration and makes sure it is turned in to the appropriate person at the church. Requests checks from financial secretary for speakers, musicians, and other needs.)

7. Registration Coordinator: _____

    (Works with appropriate staff to design registration forms, collects registration forms, and keeps event coordinator informed of numbers. Sets up registration table at the event.)

8. Decorations Coordinator: _____

    (Coordinates all decorations for the event within budget.)

Type Of Event

☐ Conference ☐ Retreat ☐ Camp ☐ Other

Event Details

Estimated number of participants: _____ Date of event: _____
Purpose of event:_____

☐ In-reach ☐ Outreach
Target Group: _____

Setting

☐ Church ☐ Camp ☐ Retreat Center ☐ Hotel Other: _____
Location for event: _____
Date secured: _____ Contact person: _____
Phone: _____ E-mail: _____

Church Calendar

☐ Date Secured   Notes _____
☐ Maintenance Notified (set up, clean up) Notes _____
☐ Media Notified: (sound, video, etc.)   Notes _____

Food

Breaks: _____

_____

Menu: _____

_____

Kitchen set up: _____

Clean up: _____

Program

Theme: _____

Theme verse: _____

Speaker

Keynote Speaker: _____

Phone: _____

E-mail: _____

Address: _____

Amount of honorarium: _____

Special needs: _____

_____

Workshop or Breakout Leaders

Workshop title: _____

Leader: _____

Phone: _____ E-mail: _____

Workshop title: _____

Leader: _____

Phone: _____ E-mail: _____

Workshop title: _____

Leader: _____

Phone: _____ E-mail: _____

Music

Worship leader: _____

Contact person: _____

Phone: _____ E-mail: _____

Amount of honorarium: _____

Special needs: _____

_____

Band or group: _____

Contact person: _____

Phone: _____ E-mail: _____

Amount of honorarium: _____

Special needs: _____

_____

Publicity

Brochures/Flyers

Person responsible: _____

Date for release: _____

Bulletin *(reaches 30 percent of church members)*

Person responsible: _____

Date to print in bulletin: _____

Newsletter/Magazine *(reaches 100 percent of the church members)*

Person responsible: _____

Date to print in newsletter: _____

PowerPoint

Person responsible: _____

Dates to show: _____

Youth Newsletter

Person responsible: _____

Date to print: _____

Newspaper, Radio, TV (only for outreach events)

Person responsible: _____

Date contacted:_____

Name of newspaper, radio station, or TV station: _____

_____

Registration

Tickets

Dates to sell: _____

Person responsible: _____

Person responsible for registration forms: _____

Registration deadline: _____

Registration at the Event

Person responsible: _____

Schedule

_____ Large Group

_____ Breakout Groups *(discussion groups)*

_____ Workshops

_____ Music

_____ Ice Breakers

_____ Fun Time

_____ Breaks *(15 minutes bathroom only, 30 minutes with food)*

_____ Decision Counselors

Follow-up

Evaluation

Person responsible: _____

Thank-you Notes

Person responsible: _____

Follow-up on Salvations/Decisions Made

Person responsible: _____

Follow-up on Prayer Requests

Person responsible: _____

Proposed Budget for the Event

Event Income

Number of paying participants . . . . . . ._____

Amount budgeted for event: . . . . $ _____

Cost per participant: . . . . $ _____

Total income:. . . . . $ _____

Event Expenses

ARRANGEMENTS

Facilities/lodging . . . . $_____

Meals. . . . . $_____

Breaks/refreshments . . . . $_____

HOSPITALITY

Packets. . . . . $_____

Photo expense . . . . $_____

Name tags . . . . $_____

Door prizes . . . . $_____

Miscellaneous . . . . $_____

PROGRAM

Honorarium– speakers . . . . $_____

Honorarium– musicians . . . . $_____

Transportation and lodging . . . . $_____

Meals for program personnel. . . . . . . $_____

Program booklet . . . . $_____

PUBLICITY

Brochures/flyers. . . . . $_____

Postage . . . . $_____

Printed materials . . . . $_____

Radio/newspaper. . . . . $_____

DECORATIONS

General decorations. . . . . $_____

Miscellaneous . . . . $_____

SCHOLARSHIPS

(This includes lodging, meals, or other fees for the following people)

Participants . . . . $_____

Program personalities . . . . $_____

Guests or coordinators. . . . . $_____

Total Income . . . . $ _____

Total Expense. . . . . $ _____

Loss/Gain . . . . $ _____

Counseling Issues
with Teen Girls

N CHAPTER SIX, we briefly discussed counseling versus mentoring and mentioned some issues teen girls face today. However, the issues they struggle with are so vast and varied that this topic warrants an entire chapter. Over the past 25 years of ministry to teenage girls, I have encountered almost every problem imaginable. At times, I knew how to provide godly counsel, but at other times, I felt hopeless because the problems were so overwhelming and complicated. Spiritual counsel has been the easiest for me over the years, but when a girl was dealing with deep psychological or emotional problems, I referred her to someone who was professionally trained to deal with those kinds of problems.

When should you refer a girl to a professional Christian counselor? That is an important question. As a leader in the girls' ministry of your church, you will be able to give wise counsel to many of their problems and guide girls through the common, everyday issues. However, there are some serious issues for which you will need to refer the girl to professional help. Knowing the difference between an everyday problem and a problem that needs help from a professional Christian counselor or a physician is essential for the following reasons:

❈ Knowing when to refer a girl to a professional Christian counselor is a legal issue. You are legally liable for advice that you give to others when you are representing the church. Letting your pastor or youth pastor know of a serious problem with a teenage girl allows him to talk with the girl's parents and refer them to the help their daughter needs. This protects not only you, but also the pastor, youth pastor, and the entire church from legal action.

114

❀ Knowing when to refer a girl to a counselor is a life-saving issue. In to-day's world, girls face life-threatening issues. Clinical depression, eating disorders, suicidal tendencies, and other self-destructive behaviors such as cutting and drug abuse can literally kill a girl. You can be a prayer warrior, encourager, and spiritual mentor to these girls, but they need the help of someone who is trained to deal with their specific problems.

❀ Knowing when to refer a girl for further help is a medical issue. I have dealt with many girls over the past years who have had medical issues that caused them to behave abnormally. Chemical imbalances, hormonal imbalances, or mental illnesses can create situations that require your attention. You may need to call a parent and say, "It might be a good idea to take your daughter for a check-up and let the doctor know that she is dealing with this problem. This could be a medical issue." Depression, overt anger, withdrawal, or mood swings can all be signs of a serious medical issue.

❀ Knowing when to refer a girl for further help is a spiritual issue. Dealing with the lives of teenage girls is not a matter to be taken lightly. James 3:1 says "Not many should become teachers, my brothers, knowing that we will receive a stricter judgment." God holds leaders more accountable, and it is necessary for women who work with teenage girls to have a close relationship with Jesus Christ and be in tune with Him. Discernment comes from the Holy Spirit. Romans 12:2 says "Do not be conformed to this age, but be transformed by the renewing of your mind, so that you may discern what is the good, pleasing, and perfect will of God." Discernment to know the difference between a spiritual issue and an issue that needs professional intervention comes from God. Often, spiritual issues need additional intervention as well.

If you give counsel to a girl who is being sexually abused and you do not report the incident, you are breaking the law. The girl who has been abused also needs professional help in order to work through the profound damage that abuse causes in a girl's heart and mind. If she does not feel that she is receiving help and being protected, she may never get over the abuse and will carry heavy baggage throughout her life. If a girl comes to you with an eating disorder or suicidal tendencies and you are not professionally trained to deal with those issues, you can cause more harm than good in that girl's life. If the girl commits suicide or dies from anorexia, then you could potentially face a lawsuit if you did not report the problem and refer the girl to a professional for help. You cannot simply tell an anorexic girl to eat. The issues are deeper than that.

As a girls' ministry leader, you can deal with spiritual issues and the normal everyday issues of a teenage girl's life. There are many Christian resources that will help prepare you to deal with these issues. These helps are listed in the back of this handbook as resources.

When you learn of some girls' behaviors or situations, be very careful in your initial response. Try not to let your mouth hang open in disbelief when facing a teenage girl who has been involved in sinful behavior. Don't overreact. Keep your composure and let the girl know you love her regardless of her behavior. God's love is not conditional on our behavior, but sin does separate us from a close relationship with Him.

Issues in Teen Girls' Lives

Many of the issues (gossip, premarital sex, guilt over sin, etc.) that teenage girls deal with on a daily basis stem from immaturity or spiritual problems. Some issues (codependent behavior, manipulative tendencies, compulsive lying, etc.) stem from generational sin passed down in their families. You will be able to deal with some of these in mentoring and discipleship small groups. Other issues, such as teen pregnancy or divorce in the family, can be dealt with in support groups (if your church is large enough). Several girls in your youth group may be dealing with the same issues and will benefit from group discussions led by a trained adult who is knowledgeable on that issue.

Sometimes, a girl may need to meet with you one-on-one, such as when dealing with guilt over sinful behavior like drinking or promiscuity. It is best to meet in a semi-private place where there are other people in the area without being close enough to hear your conversation. Good examples of semi-private locations are restaurants or a common area in your church. Never meet in a closed room where no one can see you, in a parked car, or alone in your home or the girl's home. You are only one accusation away from ruin. It will be your word against the girl's word, and you will have no defense.

In looking back over the years, the following are some of the issues I have encountered in ministering to teenage girls:

The church faces a great need in family ministry— teaching parents how to raise their children from an emotionally healthy place.

116

FAMILY ISSUES—The landscape of the family unit today is broken and bleeding from divorce; children being passed back and forth between parents; parents living together but arguing constantly; sibling rivalry and competition; drug addiction or alcoholism; mental illness; and infidelity. In fact, "In 1970, the number of single-parent families with children under the age of 18 was 3.8 million. By 1990, the number had more than doubled to 9.7 million. For the first time in history, children are more likely to reside in a single-parent family for reasons other than the death of a parent. One in four children are born to an unmarried mother, many of whom are teenagers. Another 40 percent of children under 18 will experience parental breakup."[1] These are often crippling problems for teenagers to endure. The church faces a great need for family ministry—teaching parents how to raise their children from an emotionally healthy place. I will devote an entire chapter in this handbook to parent ministry and how it is related to teenage girls. If we as ministers can get parents on the right track, we could solve many of the problems teenagers have. Dysfunctional family systems are often the root of the problems teen girls face.

More than likely, you will encounter many girls in your group whose parents are divorced. These teens are faced with a barrage of questions and fears: Why are my parents divorcing? Will I have to choose which parent I want to live with? Will I have money to do the things I want? What about my brothers and sisters? Does this mean love doesn't really last?

In many ways, divorce is much like a death, and as a minister, you should be aware of the feelings of loss that a teen might feel. He or she may be numb, shocked, angry, confused, depressed, or even suicidal. It is crucial that teens in this situation know that what they are feeling is normal. Divorce recovery support groups can be beneficial for these girls and may help them get through the rough spots. Often they feel as if they are suffering alone. Sometimes it helps to know others are experiencing the same emotions, struggles, doubts, and fears.

As a leader, you must also keep in mind that some girls are shuttled between families and cannot attend every function or event. Do not take their absence personally as a sign of failure on your part or a sign of disinterest on theirs. Be conscious in welcoming back those who have been at a noncustodial parent's home. They need to know they are welcome and accepted.

A divorced parent will often play their children against the other parent. A friend told me a story about a girl whose parents were divorced. The father was emotionally immature and needy, often looking to the girl for his own emotional support. One day, he took her out for ice cream and asked her, "Don't you love me just a little bit more than you love your mom?" The girl was devastated and rightfully so. Girls love both parents—no matter who is at fault.

Sometimes, parents refuse to change their unhealthy or sinful behavior, and you will need to help some girls cope with their life at home. This is a perfect opportunity to help them realize God is the One they can trust completely. He is their Heavenly Father and will never leave them. These girls need hope. They need to know that they can create their own godly legacy as they become adults. They will have the opportunity to make right choices even if their parents were not willing to change. For these girls, being around godly Christian families who model healthy family dynamics is critical. A friend recounted her own story of her family. Her youth minister and his wife loved on her and showed her what a godly family looked like. She said, "Before hanging out with the folks at church, I never knew that a family could be that good. All I ever knew was how my family reacted. Now I know that I can have so much more."

ABUSE: PHYSICAL, SEXUAL, EMOTIONAL—Divorce is not the only thing teen girls face. Many of them deal with some type of physical, sexual, or emotional abuse. As a leader of girls, it is important for you to recognize signs of abuse and how to take action when abuse is suspected.

1. Physical Abuse and Neglect. Physical abuse can be defined as "any act resulting in a nonaccidental physical injury, including not only intentional assault but also the result of unreasonable punishment."[2] Signs of physical abuse include the following:

- ❋ burns, bite marks, cuts, bruises, or welts in the shape of an object
- ❋ resistance to going home
- ❋ fear of adults
- ❋ acts out or destroys things
- ❋ displays violence toward other people or animals
- ❋ talks about trouble sleeping and often has nightmares.

Child neglect, which is about three times more common than physical abuse,[3] is failing to provide for a child's basic needs, such as food, clothing, shelter, and medical care. Signs of neglect include:

❀ Extreme hunger
❀ Physical fatigue
❀ Clothing unsuitable for the weather (i.e., not having a coat in winter)
❀ Apparent lack of supervision
❀ Frequent absence from school
❀ Being dirty, not bathing, presence of body odor

During my years of ministry, I have encountered some girls who did not have adequate clothing, food, school supplies, or housing. In this case, the church can step in and help. Sometimes the family is simply going through a hard time. Other times the parents are enslaved by addictions or simply do not care. In severe cases of neglect, it is important to report the situation to the authorities in your area. Again, please know the laws in your state for reporting neglect and abuse.

I remember one such girl who came to our church. She had dirty clothes that did not match, greasy hair, and she had not had a bath in quite a while. She was overweight, and her social skills were lacking. The other girls shunned her, but she was vivacious and continued to come even though the other girls had nothing to do with her. God touched a woman's heart in our church. I'll call her Laura. She reached out to the girl. She tried very hard to encourage and help the mother to no avail. The girl had never met her father; in fact, he did not even know she existed. Laura took the girl to a coin-operated laundry and taught her how to wash her clothes. She provided school clothes and camp clothes when the girl needed them. Laura even rallied people in our church to help. A man repaired the hot water heater so she could bathe regularly. Someone donated space heaters so she could be warm in the winter. Others provided Christmas presents. One day I was purchasing clothes for her with money that had been donated. I was discussing the needs of this girl with the sales clerk when a woman in the store overheard the conversation. She said, "Wait right here! Don't go away!" She ran and purchased a blanket to donate as well.

Laura worked hard teaching this teen girl manners and talked to her about the important issues in life. Soon she accepted Christ and joined a discipleship group. The other girls began to accept her, and before long she seemed like any other girl in the youth group.

I believe God had a special purpose in bringing this young lady to our church. God brought her into the path of a godly woman, and her physical, spiritual, emotional, and social needs were met. Who will she grow up to be one day? I have no idea, but I do know that God has a purpose for her life. With the help and mentoring of the people in our church, she will be able to find that purpose.

2. Sexual Abuse. One in four girls and one in ten boys will be sexually abused.[4] The National Child Protection Clearinghouse defines sexual abuse as:

"...the use of a child for sexual gratification by an adult or significantly older child/adolescent...It may involve activities ranging from exposing the child to sexually explicit materials or behaviours, taking visual images of the child for pornographic purposes, touching, fondling and/or masturbation of the child, having the child touch, fondle or masturbate the abuser, oral sex performed by the child, or on the child by the abuser, and anal or vaginal penetration of the child. Sexual abuse has been documented as occurring on children of all ages and both sexes, and is committed predominantly by men, who are commonly members of the child's family, family friends or other trusted adults in positions of authority."[5]

The availability of pornographic materials and child pornography is causing a rise in sexual abuse and rape cases. Shocking statistics are available on this subject:[6]

❀ An estimated 39 million survivors of childhood sexual abuse exist in America today.

❀ Young girls who are sexually abused are more likely to develop eating disorders as adolescents.

❀ Women who report childhood rape are three times more likely to become pregnant before age 18.

❀ An estimated 60 percent of teens' first pregnancies are preceded by experiences of molestation, rape, or attempted rape. The average age of their offenders is 27 years.

Because most girls do not report sexual abuse, it is very important for adults to recognize the signs of abuse. However, physical evidence is rare and there is often not one behavior that indicates that a girl has been sexually abused. The following behaviors may tip you off that sexual abuse has taken place:

* Depression
* Anxiety
* Nightmares
* Low self-esteem
* Running away

* An eating disorder
* Withdrawal from family or friends
* Withdrawal from usual activities
* Self-destructive behavior (i.e., cutting)
* Hostility or aggression

Many times girls who have been sexually abused demonstrate an inability to relate to men in an appropriate way. Some will flirt, sit on a guy's lap, or even engage in multiple sex acts with other teens without any sign of reservation or regret. Some dress immodestly while others wear baggy or drab clothes that do not draw attention. Many do not understand physical or emotional boundaries.

Often girls feel guilty when they have been sexually abused. The victim of sexual trauma needs to know that God in no way holds her responsible for the adult's behavior. She is not to blame.

Of course, if the perpetrator is a youth worker or church member, you must report this immediately and take action according to the laws of your state. A youth worker or church member who is a sexual predator must not be allowed to continue volunteering in the church. The likelihood of the abuse happening to another child is high.

3. Emotional Abuse. Emotional abuse can be difficult to pinpoint because it leaves no visible scars or marks. However, this is an all-too-common issue for teen girls. It is sometimes referred to as verbal or mental abuse. Emotional abuse includes:

* Yelling or screaming at the child
* Comparing the child to others ("Why aren't you more like_____?")
* Shaming or humiliating a child, especially in front of others
* Withholding appropriate physical affection, such as hugs
* Telling a child she is worthless, a mistake, bad, or no good
* Threatening or terrorizing a child

4. When Abuse is Suspected. When a girl confides in you about abuse or you suspect abuse is happening, it is important not to put words in the girl's mouth. Ask open-ended questions to gather information, such as, "Can you tell me exactly what happened?," "When did this happen?," and "How many times has this happened?" It is usually a good idea to have the girl write down exactly what happened. Do not ask leading questions such as, "Did your dad touch you in private places?" Asking leading questions will put ideas in the girl's head that may not be true. Authorities have a more difficult time in following up on or documenting a case when the victim has been asked leading questions because they have no way of knowing if the victim is telling the truth. The victim may be forced to return to the situation and could be in grave danger for telling the secret.

After the abuse has been reported and the child is in a protected situation, you may find the girl will avoid you.

Occasionally, you will encounter a girl who makes up an abuse story to get attention. If a girl begins to tell you about a situation and you feel it may be just a cry for attention, it is wise to stop her and say something like, "I want you to know that if you are getting ready to tell me about something bad that is happening to you, I may have to tell someone else in order to protect you and get the help you need." If the situation is true, the girl will more than likely continue with her story since it is a cry for help. If she is lying to get attention, she will hopefully think twice before she continues. I learned this principle the hard way.

A girl must be ready to tell the truth and stick with it before justice can be served. For example, if a girl tells you about abuse she is suffering and you report the situation to child protection services, then she must be willing to tell her story again and again when questioned by authorities. If she tells you her story and then backs out when an agent or officer questions her, then she will go back into the situation and could be in danger. This situation is very difficult to handle. That is why it is very important for you to allow the church staff to handle situations of abuse.

After the abuse has been reported and the child is in a protected situation, you may find the girl will avoid you. There usually comes a time when she regrets talking to you. She feels shame and guilt. The girl needs to be told that she did the right thing. In addition, the family may be upset with you for bringing the situation into the open. Occasionally, you will find a family member who wants to protect the perpetrator. They may have turned a blind eye to the abuse for years. The church should always be a child advocate. The perpetrator needs help as well, but the first step of action is to make sure the girl is protected. Justice must be served, and the perpetrator can be helped at a later time.

I once talked with a woman who was molested by a member of her church as a young girl. When she told what had happened, no one believed her. The man was viewed as an upstanding member of the church and was a close friend of her father. The abuse continued, and several years later, the truth was revealed. The man was sent to prison, but the girl's father continued to keep a close relationship with the abuser. The daughter felt like she was less important than her molester. She felt unprotected and carried emotional problems into adulthood caused by bitterness toward her molester and her father.

Handling abuse in the appropriate way to protect and help the victim is crucial. Most courts will mandate counseling for victims of abuse. If not, it is important to refer the victim to a professional Christian counselor for help in working through this situation. Confidentiality is of utmost importance in this type of situation. Talking to friends, other youth, other staff members, or family members is not appropriate. Telling only the person who needs to know is acceptable.

RELATIONSHIP ISSUES—Girls = relationships. Because many girls find significance and meaning through relationships (rather than accomplishments or tasks like guys do), this area of life can be tumultuous in the teen years. Gossip, mean girls, personality conflicts, and cliques are just a part of everyday life. Girls often show up at my office in tears due to a comment made about them. Talking through these issues will become a common occurrence for you. You may feel like pulling your hair out because of the way girls act sometimes, but you must guide them patiently, using the Bible as the textbook, and waiting on them to mature emotionally and spiritually. Look for teachable moments when dealing with these friendship issues.

Dating relationships are big issues as well. Broken hearts, sexual pressures, and dateless weekends are on the daily menu when working with girls. Helping teenage girls set dating standards, recognize godly character, and foster a love relationship with Jesus Christ can be helpful in solving some of these problems. It is important to help them set and keep standards, focus on friendships instead of romance, and remain accountable for their purity. By guiding them through this area, you can help prevent broken hearts and sexual pressure.

Parent/teen relationships are also an issue for teenage girls, and problems within them often stem from personality conflicts. Studying the four personality types and working with girls to educate them on personality issues are great areas of ministry. Often parents do not understand their daughter's personality, and they try to put her into a mold that does not fit her. Personality education and counseling is important in growing girls into godly young women. We will discuss parent ministry related to teenage girls in the next chapter.

BODY IMAGE AND DIETING—If you were to choose 100 teenage girls and line them up in a straight line, no two girls would look the same. However, if you asked these girls how they wanted to look, more than likely they would all have the same answer—beautiful and skinny! Teen magazines, TV, clothing styles, boys, and parents all contribute to the dilemma of negative body image in the minds of teenage girls.

A youth worker called me just last week. She had found a note on the floor at church. She picked it up to see if it was something important, and it was a letter to God from one of our teenage girls. It said:

"Dear God, I really hate what I see when I look in the mirror! I am so fat and I can't stand the way I feel when I look at other girls who are prettier than me. God, why do I have to be so ugly? What can't I be pretty like my friends?"

This youth worker was shocked. If I showed you a picture of this girl, you would think, "She's beautiful!" She is probably 5'4" tall and weighs 105 pounds. She has big brown eyes and naturally curly hair. She is gorgeous! How could she possibly feel this way? If the truth is told, many girls who will pass through your girls' ministry feel the same way.

Body image is a major issue for teen girls. Four out of five girls believe they are overweight and are dissatisfied with their bodies.[7] They constantly compare themselves to their peers, older girls, celebrities, and fashion icons, trying to be as beautiful and thin as those they aspire to be like. However, the average American model is 5'11" tall and weighs 117 pounds, while the average American woman is 5'4" tall and weighs 140 pounds. In fact, most models are thinner than 98 percent of American women.[8] Teen girls are duped into believing that the unnatural "perfection" they see before them is normal. As long as being thin is still in vogue, we will see our teenagers struggle with body image issues.

Some girls engage in unhealthy eating habits while trying to look like the women they see on TV and in magazines. While many may not reach full-blown anorexia or bulimia, many severely limit their intake of food, especially at school where their parents can't watch them, or use diet pills or plans that are not healthy for grown women, much less ones in the making. In fact, "Over one-half of teenage girls…use unhealthy weight control behaviors such as skipping meals, fasting, smoking cigarettes, vomiting, and taking laxatives."[9] Plastic surgery is on the rise among teenage girls as well. On the Internet, girls can find vast information about plastic surgery, and many are begging their parents to let them have it. Parents who are trying to boost their daughter's self-esteem give in so their daughter will feel better about herself. It is frightening how reckless girls can be with their bodies while trying to attain beauty like that of celebrities.

The average American model is 5'11" tall and weighs 117 pounds, while the average American woman is 5'4" tall and weighs 140 pounds.

Do leaders in girls' ministry contribute to the problem? Do mothers? Do fathers? The answer is yes. We don't do it intentionally, but we do it nevertheless! Our own body image sets an example in front of teenage girls. They pick up the subtle things we say and do that communicate that we are ashamed of our bodies. From this example they develop the attitude that they need to improve or change their body to look like the models on the front of magazines. Instead, they need to see godly role models who view their bodies in a positive light and treat it well by dressing modestly and maintaining a balanced approach to diet and exercise. They need to know that it's OK to want to look nice without physical appearance becoming an obsession. They need to know that God created every person uniquely. Bodies come in lots of different shapes and sizes. Those differences need to be embraced and celebrated, not scorned.

Often I hear parents say negative things about their daughters in an attempt to encourage them to do better. Guarding your speech is vital when dealing with girls. The following story illustrates this need:

> *It was a beautiful spring day and Erin was out washing her car when her dad pulled into the driveway. She had on her bathing suit and was trying to get a head start on her tan before they went to the beach for summer vacation.*
>
> *"Hi Daddy!"*

"Hey sweetheart! You missed a spot! It's at the bottom of the passenger door."

Leaning down to pick up the newspaper in the driveway and never breaking stride, he called back over his shoulder with a chuckle, "You better get to work on that diet if you want me to buy you that new bathing suit for the beach!"

Erin couldn't believe he had said that! She was fighting back the tears. Even her own dad thought she was fat! Why couldn't he just love her and not say mean things to her like that?

In her dad's mind, his comment was simply an incentive for a new bathing suit. He had heard Erin say she needed to lose weight before she went to the beach, and he was simply repeating what he had heard. But in Erin's mind, it was criticism that would stay with her the rest of her life.

How is it possible to change a girl's view of her body? We certainly cannot change what goes on in the media, what magazines print, or what others say to teenage girls, but we can keep communication open. We can model appropriate attitudes toward our own body image. We can educate parents, girls' ministry leaders, and girls on the negative influences of the media and how to counteract those influences.

Educating parents on how to help their daughters develop a more positive body image is part of parent ministry to teenage girls. Also, educating female and male youth workers on how to help girls build a better body image is a necessary part of training. Educating girls on the tactics of the media to undermine girls' view of themselves simply to make money is also a vital part of girls' ministry. An excellent Web site created by the American Family Association to keep parents and youth informed on media influences is *www.onemillionmoms.com* and *www.onemillionyouth.com*.

NUTRITION AND EXERCISE—Today's teen girls lack a healthy perspective on diet and nutrition. On one hand, restaurants are making portion sizes larger. School vending machines are loaded with junk food. PE classes have been eliminated. Girls spend hours in front of the computer. On the other hand, girls go from one fad diet to the next, suffer from eating disorders, and exercise excessively because they don't want to get fat. Girls' ministry can be the place where girls are taught that their bodies are the temple of God and that they are bought with a price and are not their own! They should use their bodies to glorify God.

Girls need to know that their physical health affects every other aspect of their lives, including their school work, their friendships, and even their relationship with God.

Eating healthy food including plenty of fresh fruits and vegetables, eating less meat and processed foods, and drinking plenty of water and less soda are all a part of glorifying God with your body. Educating teenage girls on how to eat healthy and exercise is important. Balance is the key. A friend told me about being in line at the concession stand at a volleyball game. Two thin girls were in line in front of her, trying to decide which candy had the least amount of fat and calories. One girl commented, "I'm afraid to eat that because I'll get fat." This is not a healthy view of food.

Again, balance is the key, and these topics should be woven into everything you do with teenage girls. When you have a girls' night at the church make sure you include the option of healthy food. How guilty we are in student ministry of modeling wrong eating habits with our students! Enough donuts, sodas, and pizza! I'm not talking about forever abandoning a slice of pizza for tofu sandwiches, but you can choose fresh fruit, veggies, salads, and other healthy foods that teenage girls like. Find someone in your church who understands good nutrition and get them involved in working with the girls on eating healthily.

Teenage girls love to dance around and be active to music. Start an exercise class just for teen girls! Get someone who is trained in aerobics, pilates, kickboxing, and the like to come in twice a week and get the girls moving! Sporting events for teenage girls are also good ways to get them exercising and taking care of their bodies. Playing flag football, volleyball, basketball, softball, and soccer are all ways to get girls moving. Prayer walking with a group of girls is always fun. Encourage moms and daughters to take a walk together a couple of times a week. Sometimes girls do not realize how sedentary they are until you bring it to their attention.

Moderation is the key in everything we teach teenage girls about their physical bodies. Excessive exercise, excessive eating, excessive sitting, and excessive dieting are all detrimental to the health of teenage girls.

SEXUALITY—With the onset of adolescence come questions about sexuality. Girls must navigate changing and raging hormones, the messages they receive from media, the talk over the Internet, and the input they receive from parents. Girls must make choices about several issues related to their sexuality, including whether or not to remain sexually pure. In today's culture, they must navigate the pressure to try out or accept homosexuality. They must battle a mindset that says oral sex is not really sex. The messages are multiple—and confusing. Some of these issues are discussed below.

1. Purity. Today's culture tells lies relating to a girl's sexual purity. The message is simple—sex is expected. Some researchers feel that the number of teens who are engaging in sexual intercourse has dropped in the last few years due to True Love Waits and other information on the dangers of sexual intercourse. However, girls are redefining their sexual purity to mean penile-vaginal penetration only. Anything else is fair game. Hooking up with no strings attached is an increasing trend.

Girls often send sexual messages on MySpace, add revealing or provocative pictures, and text sexual messages back and forth with guys and even other girls. Many girls use a Web cam to send sexual videos out to guys. Cybersex is often seen as a safe way to get sexual fulfillment. It is seen as a non-threatening way for girls to get the attention they crave.

The church must stand up and teach our teenage girls about the physical, emotional, and spiritual repercussions of sexual impurity. As I was finishing the final chapter of this book, a young woman in her 30s called my office. She had been in our youth group 15 years earlier. She was very adamant that she have an appointment with me the very next day. When she walked in my office and sat down, she said, "It has taken me 15 years to get the courage to talk to anyone about my past. You and your husband are greatly responsible for me being where I am today. I know many times you wanted to wring my neck and shake some sense into my head. Thank you for never giving up on me and loving me no matter what I did."

This young woman relayed to me an urgency to get her story out to teenage girls. I believe in God-appointments, and I definitely feel that this meeting was divine. Because of her standing in the community and the damage her story could do to her family, she did not want me to reveal her identity. However, she was willing to sit up most of the night to write her story so I could add it to this book and meet my deadline the next day. Here is what she wrote:

I learned many valuable lessons as a teenager. Most of them I learned the hard way. As a Christian teenager I could recite countless Scripture verses, sing numerous hymns, and explain the plan of salvation as a result of years of Sunday School lessons, church choir, Training Union, GA's, Acteens, youth retreats, quiet times, and sermons. I learned right from wrong. I could recite the Ten Commandments and the Lord's Prayer. Yet, there was something missing. I never made a decision to apply God's rules for living to my personal life. I wanted to know why I had to follow God's commandments. The concept of consequences was never in my mind. That is, until I was an adult.

Like most teenagers, I loved attention. I grew up getting lots of attention from my parents, teachers, and church leaders. As a teenager, I enjoyed the attention from guys, and I received plenty of it. Yet, there were two things I needed as a teenager that I now understand as an adult. I needed consequences for my decisions and boundaries in my life.

I was disillusioned with the concept of "safe sex." I believed that as long as I did not get pregnant or contract an STD, I could be "safe" and be sexually active with multiple partners. Never did I think about the consequences I would face 15 years later as a result of the sinful choices I made as a teenager. God protected me during the time I walked and, at times, ran away from Him.

My first sexual experience was as a 13-year-old. I had never made the decision to not allow a guy to touch me sexually. I knew God's principles, but I did not apply them to my life. So when the opportunity presented itself to receive attention from a popular guy, I allowed him to kiss me and touch me as he wanted. He made me feel special and that's what I wanted. I woke up the next morning feeling guilty, but not embarrassed. At the time there was no shame in what I did. In fact, as I began to have oral sex and sexual intercourse with numerous partners, there was no shame. I was having fun and being "safe." It seemed no one was getting hurt. Why not have some teenage fun as long as I was being careful? There was plenty of time to be serious about a relationship with "Mr. Right" when I was older. What a tremendous lie from Satan I believed. There is so such thing as "safe sex." My sexual encounters before marriage never resulted in pregnancy or the contracting of an STD, but I was not safe from the consequences of my sinful choices. Because God loved me so much, He allowed me to experience the consequences of my actions. He continues to teach me about His matchless forgiveness and love for me through that time in my life.

As a result of my sinful choices, I missed out on the blessing of giving myself to my husband completely pure and untouched. When I was engaged to the man I knew would love me completely in spite of my past, my heart ached to be able to present myself to him completely pure. Although we both had experienced God's amazing love and forgiveness for our past sins, we brought those consequences into our marriage.

As a new wife, I struggled with the memories of past sexual encounters filling my mind when I should have been completely focused on loving my husband. I was so consumed with the guilt that resurfaced, and for the first time, I was truly ashamed for the things I had done more than 10 years earlier.

I also dealt with his past sexual choices. I was consumed with comparing myself to the other women with whom he had slept. He had only a few sexual partners before we married (compared to the many I had been with), but having one sexual partner before marriage was one too many. I wanted him to only think about me, and I was terrified of not being as "good" as his past partners. In turn, without wanting to, when my husband and I would be intimate, I would think of other guys with whom I had been sexually active. I absolutely hated this! I was completely committed to my husband, and I did not want to think of anyone else but him in our marriage bed. It greatly affected our marriage, and although we were deeply in love and extremely committed to one another, our sexual pasts created a division in our marriage.

In the beginning of our marriage, I did not want to have sex with him. I did not want him to touch me. I did not want him to see my body—this body I had shared with so many others. Although I thought my past was behind me because I was forgiven for those sins, I still was in the early stages of the healing process. I viewed my husband's desire to be intimate with me as merely a physical act to fulfill his desires, so I was completely uninterested in having sex. It was several years into our marriage before I realized that sexual intercourse with my husband was much more than simply engaging in the act. He needed me to love him and show him love as his wife.

We spent months praying about our marriage and specifically about our sexual relationship with one another. We asked God to draw us closer to one another and give us an intimacy that only a husband and wife can share. Although I had given my physical body away to numerous guys over a span of several years, I had never truly given my heart to anyone. I would shut off my emotions to have momentary pleasure. Therefore, I did not deal with any emotions—including guilt—during that time. God heard our prayers and blessed us with a love and intimacy that continues to grow stronger as we work at building a Christian marriage based on God's principles.

As a teenager, I never realized that I was giving myself away to guys in ways that should have been reserved for the man I would one day call my husband. Why did my life go down the road it did as a teenager? Here are a few scattered thoughts...

My body image came from what I could do with my body, not Who created me. As a result, I saw my body as sinful, not beautiful in any way. I remember women youth leaders talking about not having sex. They would tell me that God said it was wrong. But why was it wrong? The world was telling me that I could have sex and be "safe." I needed a bigger reason to say no than "because I am a Christian." I never knew the intense pain I would later experience. That pain is still very real, but today I have the peace that comes from God's forgiveness. Only God's love and forgiveness have healed those wounds, but the scars will forever remain as a reminder of how painful life is apart from God.

My parents trusted me when I wasn't trustworthy. When I went out, they should have asked more questions about where I was going, what I was going to do, and who was going to be there. I think they thought that because I was a Christian, the temptations would not be there. But I was not exempt from any of the world's temptations that pulled me away from God. I was not prepared to handle the choices that faced me. There were so few boundaries in my life. I had always been a good girl and had done the right things. My parents thought that I always would be that perfect girl who knew right from wrong. I knew right from wrong, but I did not know how to choose right from wrong in situations that I never should have faced as a teenager. I wish I had known that being tempted was not a sin. The sin was following that temptation and not running from it.

In other words, I needed adults to be honest with me—really honest. I needed them to tell me that although God is love, He is also fair and just. I did not comprehend the concept of Him allowing me to face consequences. I needed someone to be real with me and tell me the dangers of believing the world's lies. I remember hearing how great sex is in marriage, but I don't remember hearing how my sexual relationship with my husband would be negatively, painfully affected as a result of my teenage sexual activities.

I wish teenage girls today could see my tears and the countless times I have cried myself to sleep as a married adult dealing with the painful consequences of teenage choices. To the world, I simply engaged in so-called innocent teenage fun, and the world would say there were no lasting effects of my sexual choices. Others cannot see the scars I carry, but they are deeply felt by me.

God has used our past mistakes for His glory because my husband and I have asked God to use us and our marriage to strengthen others in their relationships with God and their marriages. God has given us a passion for Christian marriages. We want to expose the lies of Satan. We want others to know and experience everything that God intended marriage to be.

In today's culture overrun with sexual references, innuendos, and even in-your-face immorality, girls need to hear stories like the one above. The church must be willing to be open, honest, and transparent about purity instead of merely sweeping the issue under the rug.

Of the 19 million new cases of sexually transmitted diseases every year, almost half of those diagnosed were between 15 and 24 years of age.

2. **Pregnancy, STDs, Abortion, and Related Issues.** One million teen girls in the United States will become pregnant over the next 12 months.[10] More than one-quarter of those pregnancies will end in abortion.[11] Of the 19 million new

cases of sexually transmitted diseases every year, almost half of those diagnosed were between 15 and 24 years of age.[12] More often than I would like, girls come to me thinking they are pregnant or that they may have a STD. When a girl confides in me, I first try to find out if she has been sexually active. (Some girls will have the wrong idea and have not even had intercourse. Never assume anything!) If she has been sexually active, it is important to find out how many monthly periods she has missed. If she has taken a pregnancy test and it is positive, then getting medical care as soon as possible is important, especially in younger girls. Letting the pastor or student minister know and informing her parents is important at this point. Again, it is wise to know the laws in your state.

Determining who talks with the parents depends on the situation and the advice of the staff member. Going with the girl to tell her parents is often advisable. Some parents respond in a helpful way to their daughters, but some do not. Talking through the situation with parents, if they are willing, at this point is important. Contacting the father of the baby is up to the girl and her family. It is good to talk with everyone involved and give them godly counsel concerning their options.

Fortunately, my city has a crisis pregnancy center that operates on Christian principles. The executive director is always willing to meet with the girl and her family. Check for a similar resource in your area and build a relationship with the personnel there. Find someone trained in giving godly counsel to guide girls in making the best choice for everyone concerned, especially the baby. Abortion should never be the preferred choice, and it is important to inform the girl and her parents of its consequences, seen and unseen.

Depending on the individual situation and your knowledge about teen pregnancy, you may need to refer the girl to a crisis pregnancy center. Make sure you are referring her to a Christian organization and not an abortion clinic. The title of an agency can be misleading. Know the laws in your state regarding age limits on sexual activity. For example, sexual activity between a boy over 18 and a girl under 16 is considered statutory rape in some states, even if the intercourse was consensual. Know the laws on parental rights and privacy as well. Most crisis pregnancy centers will have this information. If you are a lay leader, always involve the paid staff of your church when dealing with a situation of this magnitude. You may need to inform the staff and back out to let them handle the situation. Ask the person responsible for the girls' ministry if there is anything you can do and then follow what they say.

Walking through the pregnancy with the girl and the father of the baby is very important. God can use these situations to mold them into the people He wants them to be even in the midst of a bad choice. Oswald Chambers says in his book, *My Utmost for His Highest*, "If you will receive yourself in the fires of sorrow, God will make you nourishment for other people."[13]

My best friend became pregnant at age 14. She and her boyfriend went to their parents and immediately got married. In her sixth month of pregnancy, the baby was delivered stillborn. The heartache during that time was almost unbearable. She was so young and missed many of the joys that teen girls experience. With the support of their parents, the couple finished college, became successful, and now have two wonderful grown children. They have been married for more than 30 years and are godly Christians who serve the Lord. They do not broadcast their story, but they use it to help young couples in similar situations. God made them nourishment for others.

If a girl comes to you thinking she may have a sexually transmitted disease, it is important that she seek medical attention immediately. Again, know the laws in your state regarding privacy. If a girl comes with an already diagnosed STD, this is a great opportunity to counsel her spiritually and help her learn how to make better choices in her life. You may also find it beneficial to keep a file of information on STDs for girls who need to know more.

3. Oral Sex: The New Trend. Because so much emphasis lately has focused on safe sex, teen pregnancy, and the risk of AIDS, many teens are not engaging in vaginal intercourse. However, they are engaging in oral sex. "Lipstick parties" or "rainbow parties" have spread through youth culture in the last couple of years. At these oral sex parties, girls see how many colors of lipstick they can pass on to their male partners' penises.[14] Unfortunately, because penile-vaginal penetration does not occur, the girls still consider themselves virgins and think they have done nothing wrong. Some girls think oral sex is no different than kissing or fondling. They do not consider that oral sex still carries physical, emotional, and spiritual consequences. When alcohol and drugs are involved, the behavior worsens. Many girls wake up the next morning and have no idea what they have done.

You may initiate conversations with girls who have been involved in these situations. Other times, girls will get caught or feel guilty and come to you. Commonly, when parents find out about their daughter's involvement in risky behavior, they will contact their daughter's small group leader or the church staff for help. In these situations, it is still a good idea to inform the staff member over the girls' ministry and let him or her decide the course of action.

4. Sexual Identity. Movies, TV, magazines, and the news frequently promote the homosexual lifestyle as normal. Many girls do not know the truth about homosexuality. They simply believe the lie fed to them. It's an "anything goes if it feels good" culture we live in, and girls are caught floundering in this ambiguous sea. Some girls prefer not to be called homosexual, but rather "gay-ish."[15] Many girls experiment with their sexuality, dating both guys and girls to discover their sexual preference.

When girls are abused, hurt, or neglected by their dads or significant male figures in their lives, they may develop a deep hatred for men and turn to other females for close relationships. Some girls prefer to date other girls because a boyfriend has hurt them or doesn't meet their emotional needs. One girl said, "Girls understand how girls think...You can tell a girl, 'I think I'm falling in love with you' and she'll listen. A boy will slough that off, or run away."[16] They may begin to feel close to another female and mistake those feelings for romantic love or sexual attraction. As they grow older, they may begin to question their sexual identity, asking themselves if they are straight or gay.

Sometimes girls are wired as tomboys. This should never be misinterpreted as being gay. God created people with different likes and dislikes. Often this is the way God created that particular girl. Remember that God never creates someone to be gay. God will never go against His Word, which is clear about homosexual behavior. Professional, Christian counseling is important in helping girls work through these questions. As a girls' minister you will need to address this issue. Pam Gibbs' Bible study, *Designed by God: Answers to Students' Questions about Homosexuality*, is designed for a small-group setting. There are also helpful Web sites and resources that are listed in the back of this book.

Setting guidelines for girls' ministry leaders is a reality in the day in which we live. Avoiding all appearances of evil is crucial. If you see red flags with any leader, it is essential to hold her accountable for her behavior. Prolonged frontal hugging, being alone with girls, snuggling, and having close peer relationships with teenage girls are not appropriate actions for adult women. Unfortunately, some women who struggle with their sexual identity are drawn to girls' ministry. This is a growing problem the church will face.

135

Alcohol increases the chances that a teen will commit or be a victim of serious crimes, such as assault, rape, or murder.

UNDERAGE DRINKING—If you survey the activity of teens on any given weekend, there is a good chance that alcohol is involved. Over the past few years, it has become a part of the teen landscape with increasing acceptance. The problems related to underage drinking are vast and complicated, compounded by the media's influence on this age group. Lest we think that boys are the culprits, the American Medical Association released a survey in 2005 saying that teenage girls are more likely than boys to obtain alcohol illegally.

They see alcohol portrayed in a positive light with no ill effects on anyone who drinks. However, a recent Web site article stated that every three hours, a driver under the age of 21 dies in an alcohol-related car crash.[17] In fact, "drinking alcohol increases a teen's risk of death during a car crash or from drowning. Alcohol increases the chances that a teen will commit or be a victim of serious crimes, such as assault, rape or murder. It increases the likelihood that a teen will engage in risky unprotected sex. Drinking alcohol raises the chances that a teen will attempt suicide."[18] In fact, damage to the brain is real for boys and girls, and a girl who drinks is at greater risk for a bad reputation, sexual misconduct, unwanted pregnancy, or sexually transmitted diseases. Girls are also more susceptible to alcohol poisoning, hepatitis B, liver and heart disease, irregular menstrual cycles, and infertility due to the way girls' bodies processes alcohol. Teen girls need to understand why the consequences of underage drinking are so damaging. The church must help them evaluate the messages they are bombarded with in order to discern the truth. If addictive behavior such as alcohol and drug abuse continue, professional help should be sought.

Sometimes parents state they would rather their teens drink alcohol at home so they will not sneak out and drink in a dangerous place. This is legal in some states but illegal if they give alcohol to minors other than their own child. This is a growing problem the church faces: parents who allow their underage children to drink. Most parents do not approve of their teen drinking but some will model this behavior in front of their children. When their teens get into trouble or are injured, they can't understand what went wrong. Guiding parents to understand that they are role models for their children is important.

Educating girls on the dangers of drinking alcohol and using drugs is a part of girls' ministry. Breakout sessions at girls' conferences, topics for Chick Chat, and small group discipleship discussions are all excellent places to discuss the dangers of alcohol use among teenage girls.

CALL TO MINISTRY/MISSIONS—When a teenage girl wants to talk with you, do not always assume it is about a bad situation! Two years ago, a very shy girl joined my small group. She rarely talked and seemed embarrassed when I asked her to answer questions or participate. I prayed for her to come out of her shell and participate. One night after the session ended, she came up and very shyly said, "I need to talk with you. Can I call you tomorrow?" Immediately I thought, *Oh no! What has happened?* The next afternoon, I couldn't wait for her to call. I waited until I thought she was out of school and called her. We exchanged pleasantries, and I got straight to the point. "Lauren, what did you need to talk about with me?," I asked. I noticed an excitement in her voice that I had never heard before. "Mrs. Jimmie, I really believe God is calling me to be a missionary!" I was so relieved that I laughed out loud. We talked through her call to ministry, and I began to guide her in seeking God's plan for her life. To get a taste of ministry and missions, she went on a mission trip with our church, a couple of foreign mission trips, and worked with Child Evangelism Fellowship last summer. She spent a summer working for a Christian sports ministry and is in college preparing to become a missionary. What a change in this girl's life! She is no longer the shy, unassuming girl that was in my small group. She is bold in her witness and ministry because she has found God's purpose for her life.

SALVATION/ASSURANCE OF SALVATION—Sometimes a girl will come to you seeking counsel for salvation issues. Maybe she accepted Christ when she was younger and needs assurance of her salvation. Maybe she has never been saved before and is seeking a relationship with God. Leading a girl to accept Christ as her Savior is the most precious counseling you will ever do. If you have not been trained in leading a girl to Christ, talk with your pastor or youth minister. Your church may also offer classes in sharing your faith. Take the time to research Scripture related to salvation and assurance of salvation. Write those verses down and keep them in your Bible for quick reference.

Sometimes just sitting with a girl without even saying anything is a great comfort.

SICKNESS, TERMINAL ILLNESS, AND DEATH—Some girls or their family members will face terminal illnesses, death, or tragedies. In my ministry, girls have lost a mother to cancer, a father or brother in a bike accident, or a friend in a car accident. Death is an inevitable part of the human condition. God's Word is a comfort during a time of loss. During the illness or death of a family member, stop by to give the girl comfort, attend the funeral or memorial service, and continue to show concern after the funeral. Sometimes just sitting with a girl without even saying anything is a great comfort. Sending a note or bringing food or flowers is a kind gesture that the girl will remember. Allow her to grieve in her own way and on her own timetable. Remember special occasions, such as the loved one's birthday or anniversary of the death. These will be significant in the girl's mind.

It is very difficult when one of the girls in your group is terminally ill, dies, or is tragically killed. In the past three years, we have faced death in our girls' ministry more times than we have wanted.

Bethany was one of those girls. She was faithful to God in her life and had a great influence on the lives of other girls. Bethany was on a Kentucky missions trip with our youth when she became ill. We thought she had a virus. Our nurse took care of her during the week, and when she arrived home, her mother took her to the doctor. Bethany was diagnosed with acute lymphocytic leukemia.

Bethany loved missions. She went back on the mission trip the next year in the midst of chemotherapy, shortly after a bone marrow transplant. She was a trooper and never complained one time even though she did have to make a trip to the hospital to receive platelets. Bethany gave her testimony for the children at Vacation Bible School and encouraged them to accept Christ. She said, "You never know how long you have to live on this earth." Bethany never got to go back to Kentucky again, but her picture hangs on the wall of a small church in

Kentucky as a reminder to live for Christ everyday.

On the heels of Bethany's death, one of our faithful, godly college girls was tragically killed in a car accident on Valentine's Day. Brittany was a leader with our girls and had grown up in the youth group. Her ministry to her family and friends has been unparalleled. This young lady was such an awesome Christian example that our pastor preached a message after she died titled, "What Would Brittany Do?" Many young people were influenced to accept Christ and live their lives in obedience to God through that sermon.

God told me in my heart that He is going to do something that only He can do. Now is His chance. I know God will heal Hannah.

Several months later, one of the teenage girls in our ministry developed a lump on her side. After several weeks of taking antibiotics to no avail, she was diagnosed with high grade round cell sarcoma, a very rare, aggressive type of cancer. Hannah is very sick, but she is very strong in her faith. Hannah and her mother and father are very strong believers. They are already ministering to others in the hospital where she is staying in Houston, Texas. It has been amazing to see how God has used her sudden illness to change the lives of others. Young people are praying to the Father on a regular basis, some of whom have never prayed much in their lives. They are being taught to pray Scripture for Hannah, and they have seen God answer prayers in Hannah's life. God is working in their lives as they pray. Hannah's love for the Lord, as well as her parents' trust in Him, have influenced her doctors and nurses.

At one point, Hannah's doctor told her that she had a 1 percent chance to live. He informed the family that there was nothing else the doctors could do for Hannah. Her father told the doctor, "This is what we have been waiting for. God told me in my heart that He is going to do something that only He can do. Now is His chance. I know God will heal Hannah. I do not know how. He may choose to heal her from this cancer, or He may choose to give her perfect healing in heaven. But whatever He chooses, it is okay with us. We trust Him to know the best way." Several days later Hannah's blood work improved. She was taken off the respirator and began to breathe on her own. She improved enough to have her third round of chemotherapy and is now on a bland diet. We have seen miracle after miracle in Hannah's life. I do not know what God will choose to do with Hannah, but I do know that God chooses to use girls in our girls' ministries for His kingdom.

SELF-DESTRUCTIVE BEHAVIORS—Some girls deal with issues that are serious matters and need professional medical and psychological help. You can still be a spiritual mentor to these girls, but the counseling for these issues should be left in the hands of a professional Christian counselor. However, it is important for you to understand the nature and symptoms that characterize them. They are discussed briefly below.

1. Depression and Suicide. Adolescence is marked by fluctuations in mood, especially among teen girls. Changes in hormones, relationships, and cognitive function can often create temporary moodiness or sadness. This is different than clinical depression. For a doctor to diagnose depression, most of the symptoms listed below must be present for at least two weeks:[19]

* Loss of interest in normal activity
* Sleeping too much or insomnia
* Increase or decrease in weight
* Feelings of guilt or worthlessness
* Feeling sad
* Trouble concentrating
* Restlessness or irritability
* Thoughts of suicide or death

If you suspect a girl is clinically depressed (based on the symptoms listed above), it is important to talk to the girl and her parents. Depression is a serious matter. If a girl confides in you that she is thinking about killing herself, you have a legal and moral obligation to take action immediately. Find out the extent of those thoughts. Ask her pointed questions such as, "How long have you been thinking about this?" "Have you written a note?" "Do you have a plan in place for killing yourself?" Inform your pastor, youth minister, and the girls' parents. Do not take such comments lightly. They are often cries for help and, if left unanswered, may send the girl spiraling downward even further.

2. Eating Disorders. While virtually all girls struggle with their body image at some point in their lives (especially in the teen years), some girls face a greater struggle with an eating disorder. Eating disorders are classified in several categories and carry different warning signs:

Anorexia nervosa is characterized by self-starvation and excessive weight loss. Some signs of this problem include: a refusal to maintain a normal body weight for height, body type, and age; obsession with body weight and shape; fear of weight gain or being "fat"; feeling "fat" despite dramatic weight loss; loss of menstrual periods; eating only in tiny portions, alone, or in a ritualistic fashion; and always having an excuse for not eating.

Bulimia nervosa is a secretive cycle of binge eating followed by purging. A person will eat large amounts of food in short periods of time, then get rid of the food through vomiting, laxative abuse, or over-exercising. Some signs include: episodes of bingeing and purging; self-induced vomiting, abuse of laxatives, diet pills and/or diuretics; excessive exercise or fasting; frequent dieting; obsessive concern with body weight and shape; depression following a binge; preference for high-fat, high-calorie food during a binge; unusual swelling of the cheeks; calluses on the back of the hands and knuckles from self-induced vomiting; and discoloration or staining of the teeth.

The causes of eating disorders are as varied as the girls who suffer from them. However, people with this problem often use food as a way of coping with feelings and emotions that seem overwhelming. It provides a sense of control. Other contributing factors include (but are not limited to): low self-esteem, depression, anxiety, feeling out of control, trouble in family or personal relationships, and a history of being teased about weight or size.

If you suspect that a girl is suffering from an eating disorder, take appropriate action. Talk to your pastor and the girl's parents or guardian. Girls in this situation need professional help. Experts in eating disorder treatment have found that immediate professional help significantly increases a girl's chances for recovery.

3. Self-mutilation. A disturbing trend among teen girls is self-mutilation. Also called self-inflicted violence, self-harm, cutting, or self-abuse, it is the act of "attempting to alter a mood state by inflicting physical harm serious enough to cause tissue damage to one's body."[20] This may involve carving, scratching, biting, bruising, hitting, picking or pulling at skin or hair, burning, or branding one's body. The purpose is not to kill oneself. Rather, people who engage in self-harm are trying to relieve otherwise unbearable emotional stress, much like a person with an eating disorder. While the act is painful, it reduces tension and emotional distress and may lead to a calm state.[21] Others report that they want to hurt themselves to feel something, even if it is pain, because they feel numb.[22]

Many people who injure themselves struggle with a past trauma such as sexual, emotional, or physical abuse. Depression, impulsivity, hopelessness, aggression, trouble with parents, and feeling invalidated are also factors. Warning signs of this behavior might include: wearing long-sleeved shirts or long pants in warm weather (to hide marks or cuts); unexplained cuts or burns; difficulty in handling emotions; and a refusal to engage in activities that might reveal the skin (such as going swimming).[23] As with other high risk behaviors, if you suspect a girl is harming herself, take action. Talk to the girl, her parents, and the appropriate church staff members.

Taking Care of Yourself

Mentoring teenage girls can be stressful. Problems can seem overwhelming and hopeless. Sometimes you will need to get away and spend intimate time with God in order to be refreshed enough to continue on in your ministry to teen girls. Allow Him to fill you up in order to pour yourself out to girls. Spend time with God. Spend time with your family. Then go back and spend time with girls. Ministering to teenage girls can be a 24/7 job, but it is important to take time to renew and refresh yourself in order to make a difference in the lives of girls.

Ministry to Parents of Teen Girls

MINISTRY DESIGNED TO INVOLVE PARENTS in the lives of teenagers has been the focus of many youth ministry conferences in recent years. Churches are beginning to recognize that parents are responsible for the spiritual teaching and training of their sons and daughters, and the church is to be a helper in that process. Until recent years, that principle was somewhat reversed. With the development of youth ministry in the '50s and '60s, churches designed separate programs for youth, segregating student ministry from the overall church. It became easier and easier for parents to place the responsibility of their teen's spiritual development on the church.

Because teens are often segregated from the rest of the church in an activity-based student ministry, many who were faithful in church attendance during middle school and high school do not attend church after they graduate. Many feel out of place because they have not established relationships or links to the overall church program. They feel displaced and drift from the church entirely. A survey of 3,680 college students conducted by the Higher Education Research Institute of UCLA found that between their final year before college and junior year in college, frequent religious service attendance dropped from 52 percent to 29 percent.[1]

Today, however, a paradigm shift is taking place, and more churches are seeing the need to involve students in the ministry of the entire church, not just youth ministry activities. More churches are educating parents in becoming the primary spiritual leaders for their sons and daughters. Student ministry with a strong family ministry emphasis is important. Teenagers need it, and parents want it. God is stirring hearts to make it happen.

In this chapter, we will discuss parent ministry as it relates to teenage girls. The following are all part of parent ministry:

* Fostering father/daughter relationships
* Improving mother/daughter relationships
* Assisting families in building better communication skills
* Teaching parents to set healthy boundaries for their daughters
* Teaching parents to grow spiritually and model that growth for their daughters (This is part of the overall church program, but it is also the responsibility of girls' ministry.)
* Teaching parents to communicate spiritual truths and how they apply to their daughters' life
* Teaching parents to help their daughters make wise decisions

Having a sense of family is one of the greatest needs of a teenage girl, so churches must be intentional about fostering deeper relationships between girls and their parents. As we discussed in chapter seven, there are many opportunities for girls and their parents to grow together. Not only do they need opportunities to learn together, but they also need opportunities to learn about each other separately. Workshops, seminars, Bible studies, and parenting classes can meet these needs.

Fostering Father/Daughter Relationships

The father/daughter relationship has been the subject of innumerable scientific studies, ranging from a father's influence on a girl's virginity to her activity in high risk behaviors. The results are similar across the board—the influence of a caring, nurturing, proactive father provides a strong foundation for a girl's future success. One study concluded that girls who have a healthy relationship with their parents were "46 percent less likely to use drugs, 27 percent less likely to use alcohol, and 52 percent less likely to skip school."[2] Another study indicated that girls who have a good relationship with their fathers wait longer to have sexual intercourse. Girls with a poor relationship with her fathers were nearly twice as likely to lose their virginity over the course of a year than girls with a good relationship with their fathers.[3] In a similar study, one girl stated, "I didn't seek acceptance from other guys because I got it all from Dad. And I got just as much attention as I needed. And I didn't feel like I needed to go seeking acceptance from guys. But I think if my Dad wasn't a part of my life, I would have been a lot more interested in boys."⁴ While some fathers struggle to relate to their daughters as they mature into adolescence, it is clear that their influence impacts teen girls.

An additional issue growing more prevalent is the rise of blended families. This family dynamic leaves stepfathers struggling to know how to relate to their stepdaughters, and most feel even more awkward than biological fathers. When I ask girls about their relationship with their stepfather, they will often reply, "I don't have a relationship with him." Of course, it is an awkward situation for both. Because of the rise in sexual abuse in America, stepfathers are often under a cloud of suspicion when they try to develop a relationship with their stepdaughters. It is a difficult situation, and the church can guide stepfathers to know how to have an appropriate relationship with their stepdaughter.

All of a sudden, daddy's little girl is a budding young woman. Many fathers feel awkward at this stage of their daughter's life. They either go overboard in teasing their daughters about becoming a woman, or they back off completely and say or do nothing because they don't know what else to do.

When offering training opportunities for parents, it is important to teach dads how to relate to their daughters during puberty. All of a sudden, daddy's little girl is a budding young woman, and many fathers feel awkward at this stage of their daughter's life. They either go overboard in teasing their daughters about becoming a woman, or they back off completely and say or do nothing because they don't know what else to do. Some don't want to engage in physical play like wrestling or basketball because they are afraid of hurting their daughter. The tomboy has been replaced by a china doll. However, it is important for fathers to know that their daughters need them more than ever before during this difficult stage of growth.

Seminars for fathers might include topics such as: what changes to expect during adolescence; how to really listen to your daughter; how to get involved in your daughter's life; how to take your daughter on dates; how to know when your daughter is ready to date; how to set boundaries for teen girls; how to encourage your teen's potential; how to be Web-savvy in a high-tech world, as well as an open discussion forum with other fathers of teen girls. Focus on things girls want their fathers to know. This will be discussed later in the chapter.

Conferences for girls should focus on helping them understand their dads and learning to communicate with them on a deeper level. Girls must learn how to relate to their families in a more mature fashion. They must learn conflict resolution, compromise, and dealing with their emotions. They need to learn how to communicate their thoughts and feelings so their parents will understand and respond. (A shouting match, slamming doors, and sarcasm generally won't produce the results they want!).

A seminar could also help a teenage girl realize that sometimes she may picture God the same way she sees her daddy. If a girl has a father who is harsh and legalistic, she will often see God in the same light. If she has a dad who is distant and uninvolved in her life, she may picture God the same way. It is important to teach teenage girls that their earthly fathers should give them a taste of God's love for them, but sometimes they falter in mirroring God's love. Girls need to know that God's love is the only thing that will truly fulfill them.

Improving Mother/Daughter Relationships

Nothing is like the relationship between a mother and her daughter. When she is young, a daughter plays dress up in her mommy's clothes, shoes, and jewelry. She might even attempt to smear on mommy's lipstick. That loving admiration disappears when adolescence hits, and suddenly, "mommy" is replaced by the single phrase, "Oh, Mooooooooooooommm" (insert dramatic, disgusted, frustrated, irritated voice here). These dramatic and drastic changes in a girl at the onset of adolescence can mystify and devastate a mother. Many mothers may find themselves wondering, *What happened to that loving, caring, helpful child? Who are you and what have you done with my daughter?*

Mothers need reassurance that what they're going through is completely normal. This conflict arises because a girl is searching for her own identity apart from her parents, in particular her mom. She's asking herself, *Do I want to be like my mom? Do I want to be different? How can I be different?* A girl needs to know that her mother (and father) will accept her as a coming-of-age adult. She needs to know that she is loved and accepted, even if her thoughts, values, and opinions differ from those of her mother.

Even though most mothers can identify with their daughters simply because they are both females, they still need help in understanding youth culture and the pressures their daughters face. They need help in being the mother their daughter needs.

Mother/daughter banquets, mother/daughter conferences, prayer groups and Bible studies for mothers, spa days to pamper mothers and daughters, and mother/daughter shopping trips are all ideas that can improve the relationships between mothers and their daughters.

Spiritual Transformation of Parents

I often hear parents say, "Parenting is hard because there is no handbook on how to raise your children!" Actually, God has given us a complete manual on child rearing—the Bible. Throughout the Bible, God has provided examples of good parenting and bad parenting.

His Word teaches parents to live pure and holy lives and to model that for their children. Providing opportunities for parents to engage in Bible study, worship, and prayer will help them to encounter God and be spiritually transformed. When the parents' daily walk matches their talk, their daughters will be more apt to choose a growing relationship with God for themselves. Research shows that the church attendance of parents is a good predictor of whether their children will attend church in their young adult years. Teenagers whose mothers "attended church once a month or less during their teenage years go to church less often during their young adult years."[5]

In her book, *Your Girl: Raising a Godly Daughter in an Ungodly World*, Vicki Courtney talks about parents leaving a legacy of faith for their children:

"One of the most important things we can leave our daughters is a heritage of faith. Probably the biggest determinant is whether we...model to them what having faith in Jesus looks like...It is one thing to verbalize our belief in Christ to our daughters but quite another to act upon that belief...

"Are you modeling a sincere faith in Christ to your daughter? Are your actions and attitudes consistent with your expressed belief in Jesus? If not, your daughter could be left with the impression that faith in Christ is not a serious matter."[6]

When a parent accepts Jesus Christ into their lives and begins to live in a way that is pleasing to God, they will be better parents. As the Holy Spirit guides the parents, they will be able to make right decisions in parenting their daughters. God will give them discernment, and they will be able to better help their daughters apply Scripture to their everyday lives.

What Daughters Want Parents to Know

Even though teenage girls may not be able verbalize the following ideas, there are some things they want their parents to know. These will be valuable topics for classes, newsletter articles, parent retreats, banquets, and discussion groups:

1. TEENAGE GIRLS NEED THEIR DADS TO BE INVOLVED IN THEIR LIVES—
Every female has the deep need for a male to love, cherish, and protect her. A girl's father is an earthly picture of God. What pictures do teenage girls have of God based on the character and actions of their earthly fathers?

My husband and I were very blessed in raising our daughter. Ginger is 31 years old now and never really experienced a rebellious stage in her life. I believe this was largely due to the fact that my husband spent significant time with her during her childhood and teen years. Once a week as she was growing up, they went out to breakfast together.

A girl's father is an earthly picture of God.

On her last day of high school, my husband picked her up at school for a special date. She would walk across the stage that night at graduation, and a new chapter of life would begin. Feeling a little nostalgic, he asked Ginger to reminisce with him about her favorite thing that she remembered doing in her life. She could have picked anything because we traveled a lot and enjoyed many fun times together as a family. However, without hesitation, she replied, "Going to get a biscuit with you every Wednesday morning at the 'tin man shop.'" Chuckling, he said, "No, honey, I mean the *best* thing." She repeated unwaveringly in her "Dad, you're not listening to me" voice, "Going to get a biscuit with you every Wednesday morning at the 'tin man shop'!"

Let me explain. The "tin man shop" was a little shop in downtown Stone Mountain that sold eccentric items for the patio and yard. A bigger-than-life-size suit of armor stood hideously guarding the front door. That's why Ginger called it the "tin man shop." Surprisingly, in addition to yard items, they sold pastries, muffins, and biscuits. Ginger and Sam stopped there every Wednesday morning, picked up a biscuit, and went to Stone Mountain to spend some time together before school.

That day, Sam realized that it wasn't the expensive or elaborate things that were important to his daughter, but rather the simple pleasure of spending time together. They both had a good cry that afternoon thinking back over those memories, but they soon dried their tears, took off to get a biscuit at the "tin man shop," and spent the afternoon at Stone Mountain.

2. TEENAGE GIRLS NEED A STABLE FAMILY ENVIRONMENT—Girls need to know there is mutual caring and intimacy without the fear of rejection in their families. The home needs to be a safe haven where they can escape when everyone else is against them. To the contrary, many homes are a battleground and no safer than any other place teen girls have been throughout the day. Often families do not spend time eating a meal together, listening to one another, or talking about what is going on in each other's lives. Busy lives force most families to eat at the drive-thru or eat separately several nights a week.

Many homes are a battleground and no safer than any other place teen girls have been throughout the day.

Often when there is not a caring, stable environment at home, teens will find more and more excuses to not go home. One girl told me that she works as many hours as she can, goes to the library, and even drives around in her car just to keep from going home because the environment there is so hostile and stressful.

The following is a profile of a postmodern teenage girl who does not have a stable family life. The possibilities of the following scenario are shocking but very real in youth culture today.

LAUREN turned her MP3 player up as loud as it would go and logged onto Instant Messenger. She couldn't bear the screams coming from the den any longer. Her mom and dad had been arguing for hours. Mom was accusing Dad of looking at women on the Internet, and Dad was accusing Mom of being a nag. When would they grow up and stop acting like children? As she scanned her list of buddies, there he was—her dream guy! At first his words on the computer scared her a little, but she got used to it. He made her feel loved and important.

At least he didn't act like her dad! He showed her how much he loved her. They spent time on the computer every night. She knew it was wrong to have sex before marriage, but she didn't consider the things they did and said while on the Internet as having sex. Somehow it made her feel like she didn't have a problem in the world the minute she turned on the Web cam. Sometimes the things he asked her to do made her feel a little strange, but she was willing to overlook that. He loved the way she looked and told her how beautiful she was. Having an older guy think she was beautiful made her feel very special. She said and did things that made him feel really good. She had found something she was good at, finally! No one else knew, and her parents were preoccupied anyway. She was always sure to lock her door, and besides, she would probably never meet him in person anyway.

The thought of this situation happening to their precious daughter is a nightmare to parents, but the possibility of girls being drawn into unhealthy relationships is very real, especially when their love bank isn't being filled by their parents. Parents must provide a stable family life to protect their daughters from the dangers of the world today.

3. A Girl's Mother Is the Number One Influence in Her Life—Teenage girls need mothers who will show them by their everyday actions how to be godly women. They don't need friendship with their mother; they need a mother who will be the adult and provide guidance and boundaries to protect her daughter as she goes through the teenage years. Unfortunately, many mothers are reliving their own teen years vicariously through their daughters. Some even dress like them, thinking that their daughters might view them as cool or popular.

Mothers have more influence on their daughters than anyone else. Girls are subconsciously watching mom to learn how to become a woman, wife, and mother. Most moms do not believe they have a significant amount of influence over their daughters, but they do.

4. TEENAGE GIRLS NEED MOM AND DAD TO LOVE EACH OTHER—This is a critical issue today in our society. Girls have a deep desire for the fairy-tale family. You may laugh at the thought, but God actually planned it that way from the beginning. Unfortunately, because of our sinful nature, we will never have the perfect fairy-tale family. But nevertheless, the hearts of little girls desire a happy, peaceful, loving family. They desperately long for Mom and Dad to get along and have a peaceful relationship.

My 2½-year-old granddaughter has taught me much about the desires of a girl's heart. She adores her daddy and would rather be with him than anyone on the earth. She would choose him over her little friends, her mommy, or even her MiMi! Her favorite movie to watch is a clip of a little girl and her mommy and daddy on a Barney video. The little girl falls asleep on the sofa, the mom and dad come in and sing, "I love you, you love me, we're a happy family…" Then daddy scoops her up in his arms and carries her up to bed, while mommy walks beside them, carefully tucking the blanket around her daughter. My granddaughter watches this clip over and over, and each time she watches it, she bursts into tears, not knowing how to control the emotion she feels when watching this touching moment. Did someone teach her to feel that way as a 2½-year-old? No! God put those desires for a loving family in her heart as a little girl, and they will remain the same until the day she dies.

Parents need to be more concerned about doing the right thing than worrying about what the other parent is doing wrong. They need to focus on their daughter's welfare, not proving which one is right.

Even if the parents have divorced and the marriage cannot be restored, parents should still love each other. That may sound bizarre to you. How can two people who cannot save a marriage (and possibly hate each other) still love each other? Let me explain. I am not suggesting romantic love, but rather godly love. Godly love is an action, not a feeling. First Corinthians 13 says that love is patient and kind. It does not envy, boast, or act improperly. Love is not selfish or easily angered and keeps no record of wrongs. Love does not delight in evil, but it rejoices in the truth. A divorced couple can be patient with each other. They can be kind to each other. They should not be rude to each other. They can show respect in their actions toward each other for the sake of their daughter. Parents need to be more concerned about doing the right thing than worrying about what the other parent is doing wrong. They need to focus on their daughter's welfare, not proving which one is right. This may be a foreign idea to most divorced couples, but if they can grasp this concept, it will change their daughter's life.

5. Teenage Girls Need for Mom And Dad to Respect Each Other—

Often one parent will criticize the other parent in front of their daughter. Mistakenly, they think this will bring the daughter to their side of the relationship or make the daughter love them more. In reality, sooner or later it will cause the daughter to lose respect for the critical parent.

Our daughters are smarter than we give them credit for sometimes, and they easily figure out the truth. Most of the time, teens are already aware of the character flaws in their parents. If not, it will be better to let them discover truth on their own and not get caught in a verbal war between their parents.

Fathers need to recognize the major role they play in their daughters' lives and accept the God-given responsibility to model Christlike behavior.

6. Girls Learn from Their Fathers what a Husband and Father Looks Like—

She will either want a husband just like her dad, or she will say, "I never want to marry a man like my dad!" For example, if a father treats his wife with respect, a daughter notices. If he opens car doors for women and brings flowers home for his wife just because he loves her, his daughter learns that women are to be loved and respected. On the other hand, sometimes a father's actions will cause a girl to view herself and men in a negative light. If a father abuses his family verbally or physically, a daughter learns that women are to be treated as property and not treasured. Fathers need to recognize the major role they play in their daughters' lives and accept the God-given responsibility to model Christlike behavior.

7. **Teenage Girls Don't Need to Be Told what to Do**—As a girl works through adolescence, one of the tasks she must learn to master is the ability to make good decisions by thinking critically about the choices before her. A "do as I say because I said so" mentality does not foster a sense of independence or confidence in making wise choices. On the contrary, it creates teenage girls who are prone to peer pressure. They don't know how to think for themselves. Some parents consistently tell their daughters what to do and what not to do, but they never teach them how to think through situations and make right decisions. When away from their parents and a peer tells them to take a drink or use drugs, they do it because they do not have the skills to think through the choices and make wise decisions. The church needs to teach parents to use God's Word as their guideline in teaching their daughters to think critically through the situations they will face so they can develop mature decision-making abilities.

Words are spoken once but remembered for a lifetime.

8. **Daughters Need Their Parents to Guard Their Words**—Words are spoken once but remembered for a lifetime. Parents need to think before they speak and should never use words they will regret. Phrases and labels such as "stupid," "clumsy," "dumb," and "fat" can all turn into self-fulfilling prophecies in a girl's life. A parent's positive words to a daughter are like a wall of protection around her heart and self-esteem. Positive encouragement protects her. Criticizing her looks, actions, friends, or clothes are all a blow to her self-esteem.

When they are critical, verbally abusive, and negative, they pass a legacy of words down to their daughters. This sin can be passed down for generations. On the other hand, they can pass down a legacy of words that are loving, kind, uplifting, positive, and encouraging to their daughters. Often parents need help in breaking the cycle of generational sin that has been passed down to them, but they can break the pattern and change the course of their family forever.

9. **Teenage Girls Never Want to Be Compared to Others**—God created teenage girls as individuals. Each one has her own unique personality, skill set, and emotional make-up. There is no other person exactly like her. Parents can learn to accept their daughter for the person God made her to be.

Often mothers will say something like, "When I was your age, I weighed 98 pounds" or "When I was in high school, I was elected 'Most Popular' three years in a row" or "I always made straight A's in school. I don't know why you can't." Think how this will make the girl feel to be compared to her mother in looks, popularity, and intelligence. She feels that she does not measure up: *I don't even look as good as my mother! I'm not as popular. I'm not as smart as I should be.*

Parents often have difficulty not comparing their children to each other. Innocent remarks comparing grades, talents, looks, or personalities of siblings will be remembered and resented for a lifetime. The church should teach parents to encourage each child to live up to the potential God has given him or her but never compare them to anyone else. Each is a unique individual.

While a girl desperately needs unconditional love, she also needs her parents to recognize her good character, qualities, and abilities.

10. **Teen Girls Need Their Parents' Unconditional Love**—A girl needs acceptance from her parents because she is their daughter, not because of what she does or what she looks like. Often, girls will excel in sports but neglect other areas of their lives, even their spirituality, just to please her parents. Sometimes girls will put undue pressure on themselves to make perfect grades. If they make anything less, they are afraid their parents will not love them as much. Most of the time, these are inaccurate feelings, but nevertheless they are real. Often girls will starve themselves because of careless comments made about her looks. Teaching parents to think about their comments, body language, and actions toward their daughters may be the key to helping their daughter become the well-rounded young lady that God plans for her to be.

While a girl desperately needs unconditional love, she also needs her parents to recognize her good character, qualities, and abilities. Parents need to learn how to sincerely compliment their daughters about the good things they observe them doing, such as being kind to someone, telling the truth, and helping someone who is elderly or in need.

11. **Teenage Girls Need Time to Talk About Problems**—Set up a specific time and place to discuss difficult issues like bad grades, coming in after curfew, and other necessary but potentially explosive topics. Having coffee, tea, or hot

chocolate is a good idea. When the drink is hot, talk. When it gets cold or is gone, stop discussing the problem. Don't carry your problems throughout the whole day. Let your daughter know that you are concerned about her problems and that you will work through issues and discipline problems, but they have nothing to do with the fact that you love her and want to have a happy family life.

12. Girls Need Their Parents to Laugh and Have Fun with Them— Parents need to be able to laugh and have fun with their daughter. Parents need to learn how to prioritize their time. We all have work to do and problems in life to deal with, but parents need to discipline themselves to put the work and problems aside and do something they will enjoy with their daughters. Your church can provide opportunities for families to have fun together. Sometimes I think this is as spiritual as anything else we can do.

Parents need to be able to laugh and have fun with their daughter.

Daddy/daughter dates are a great way to show her that she is special. A dad's undivided attention is important to a teenage girl. She needs for him to listen to her talk about all the things that may seem trivial to him but are important to her. If he listens to the trivial things, then she will come to him with the important things as well. Going out to breakfast once a week is a good plan.

Mother/daughter times together are also important. Girls need for their moms to listen, too. If a mom listens to the silly things her daughter has to say while she is growing up, then the daughter will be more prone to talk to her mom when faced with a serious problem. Often on MySpace.com there is a question on a girl's profile: "Who is the number one person you talk to about your problems?" It is pretty easy to guess which girls will answer, "My mom." It is usually those who have a good listener for a mom.

Shopping for clothes can be a fun activity for moms and daughters, but it is often stressful. Teenage girls want to keep up with fashion and will want to buy clothes that are unacceptable in the mother's opinion. The church needs to teach mothers to be discerning in this area and to choose their battles wisely. A girl may pick clothes that are simply unattractive to the mother. If there is nothing sensual or inappropriate about the article of clothing, she might want to consider holding her tongue for a more important issue. Other mother/daughter activities include walking or exercising together, going out for lunch, attending fashion shows, or getting together with another mother/daughter pair for dinner and a movie. It can also be fun to stay home, put on your pajamas, snuggle up, and watch a chick flick together!

A girl may pick clothes that are simply unattractive to the mother. If there is nothing sensual or inappropriate about the article of clothing, she might want to consider holding her tongue for a more important issue.

13. **Teenage Girls Need Dad to Be the Spiritual Leader**—Postmodern girls will not respond well to legalism, but they will respond to a godly father who loves and protects his family. Sometimes mothers with strong personalities will take on the leadership of the family. Because opposites attract, the husband will often have a more laid-back, easy-going personality. In this situation, I often hear mothers say, "I have to be the head of the family because he won't!" Many times daughters in a family like this will be confused and rebellious. The greatest thing a mother can do is be submissive and encourage her husband to be the leader of the family. The greatest thing a dad can do is step up to lead and protect his family the same way Jesus loves and protects the church.

Throughout my years in youth ministry, I have seen a common occurrence in every church I have served. There were many opportunities for youth to go away on camps, retreats, and mission trips. There is something special about getting away for intense Bible study and worship and focusing on God, resulting in a mountaintop spiritual high. When they arrive home, the students' parents have not had that same experience. More often than I would like to admit, I have seen arguments between parents and their teens in the parking lot after a youth trip. The parents do not realize what God has done in their daughter's life during the trip. The parents have not had the mountaintop experience, and more than likely, they have not grown spiritually at the same level as their daughter during that week. The girl experiences a spiritual high, and when she gets home, she levels off on a higher plane than before. Parents often put out the fire the Holy Spirit has ignited, causing the girl to regress in her relationship with God. Focusing on family ministry and giving parents and their daughters opportunities to grow together is important. I'm not saying that parents need to be at every event their daughter attends, but there should be ample opportunities at church and outside events for them to experience God and grow together.

14. TEEN GIRLS NEED BOUNDARIES FOR THEIR OWN PROTECTION— Peer pressure is overwhelming, and teenage girls need a way out of temptation. I believe it is the parents' responsibility to provide that escape route. She may try to push the boundaries, but she really needs to know they are firm. Boundaries create a sense of security for girls. Her parents need to set up the boundaries and consequences behind closed doors until they fully agree, and then with an undivided front, let her know the boundaries. She needs the boundaries to be consistent but carried out with grace when necessary. Praying for God's discernment and leadership is necessary in knowing the difference.

In setting boundaries for daughters, it is important for parents to choose their battles carefully. Here are important questions to ask:

❀ *Does God's Word provide guidance or instruction about this situation?* Some issues are simply right or wrong. The Bible addresses those situations. For example, believers are not to develop intimate relationships with non-believers. This issue may surface for a teen girl who wants to date a non-Christian. Setting up boundaries based in God's Word is important in teaching and training daughters. Often, girls today do not recognize truth found in Scripture. Parents need to teach their daughters that God's Word is completely true and is the authoritative guide for life. This is a battle worth fighting.

❀ *Does this issue threaten or harm the well-being of my daughter?* Will this activity put my daughter in danger or hurt her emotionally in the future? Setting boundaries for dating, driving, curfew, and the like are issues that can protect your daughter's safety and well-being.

❀ *Is this issue illegal?* We don't even consider that setting boundaries for our daughters sometimes involves legal issues. For example, drinking alcohol is illegal in the United States for anyone under the age of 21. We often think of this as a personal conviction, when actually it is a legal matter as well. In some states, driving after 8 p.m. is illegal for a person with a restricted driver's license. Parents will sometimes ignore this law out of convenience. What does this teach their daughter?

❋ *Does my decision teach my daughter how to be a mature, godly young lady?* There should be a healthy balance when setting boundaries for our daughters. Often parents will go to an extreme. A messy room is OK occasionally if it is not a health hazard. An occasional B on the report card doesn't mean a girl is a failure. Not making the starting line-up teaches a girl to work toward a goal. These issues should not be a daily battle between parents and their daughters.

❋ *Is this issue simply about my personal choice?* Often parents try to force their personal preferences on their daughters, and this is where much of the conflict surfaces. Girls may choose clothing, hairstyles, jewelry, room decorations, and other things that a parent simply does not like. If there is nothing immoral, illegal, or unbiblical about the clothing or preference, then this is a battle to avoid. Other things are more important.

15. PARENTS NEED TO PRAY FOR THEIR DAUGHTERS.— Parents need to be taught to pray for and with their daughters. They should pray that God will protect her mind, heart, and body; that she will recognize evil and walk away from it; and that she will know truth and embrace it. Parents should also pray for their daughter's future husband, her salvation, that God will put people in her life who will influence her to grow to be a godly woman, and that she will recognize God's plan for her life on a daily basis.

Parents should not only pray for their daughters, they should pray with their daughters. It may seem a little weird at first, but they will soon get used to it and begin to go to their parents for prayer. There is something comforting about hearing someone pray for you, especially your parents! It just may give her the confidence to make it through the day.

I recently went on a mission trip with our youth. We did Vacation Bible School at a church, and I was cleaning up the kitchen after we served a snack to the children. One little girl came in and asked for something to drink. While I was pouring her drink, she said, "I can't come to church tomorrow. I have to go to the doctor." I told her I was sorry she was not feeling well and asked if I could pray for her. Her eyes lit up, and I put my hands on her shoulders and prayed that God would help her to feel better and bless her. She left, and a few minutes later, another little girl came in and said, "My grandpa is real sick." She stood there silently, looking at me with questioning eyes. It took me a second to catch on, but then I realized what she wanted. I said, "Would you like for me to pray for him?" She nodded her head adamantly. This same scenario went on for 15 minutes. I prayed for dads in jail, for kitty cats that were lost, for moms that were using drugs, for a brother that had been in an accident, and on and on. Every time I would finish praying, another child would be standing there ready with a request. When we got in the van that night to leave, one of the ladies in our group said with a smile on her face, "A little girl came up to me tonight and said, "You got anything you need prayed over? There's a lady in the kitchen that will pray right there on the spot!"

It was a humorous moment, but then it dawned on me that some children and youth have never known the privilege of having someone pray for them. I wondered if any of those children had ever known that privilege before that day. Those children were hungry for someone to pray for their needs. Parents need to realize how comforting their prayers are to their daughter and how a parent's prayer can literally change the course of their daughter's life.

Personality Issues for Parents & Daughters

Many of the problems between parents and their daughters stem from personality conflicts. When parents come into my office to address relationship problems with their daughters, I talk them through personality issues. Addressing this with their daughters is also necessary.

Teaching parents to understand their personalities and what causes them to react in certain ways will not only help them to get along better with each other, but it will help them to understand their daughter as well. Teaching parents to raise and respond to their daughter according to her personality will lessen conflict in a family. Teaching girls to understand their parents' personalities will help her to have a better relationship with them. Personality training books and programs are listed in the Internet resources section of this handbook.

Keeping Girls Safe from Digital Dangers

Teenage girls are sitting ducks on the Internet. During the last year, there has been much hoopla over MySpace.com and the information girls are putting on the Web for anyone to see. Predators are combing the Internet to find an easy target. Girls have no idea the danger in which they put themselves. Here are a few pointers for helping parents keep up with technology:

- ❉ *Provide computer classes and demonstrations for parents.* Teach them how to get on the Internet, how to look up profiles on MySpace.com, and how to check their daughter's IM activities. Showing parents how to check the history on their daughter's computer is not an invasion of privacy; it is a safety net for the lives of our precious girls.

- ❉ *Keep parents informed.* Make sure they are aware of new trends in technology. An excellent resource for parents is The Center for Parent/Youth Understanding (*www.cpyu.org*).

- ❉ *Encourage parents to talk with their daughters about the dangers of the Internet and to give them tips on how to be safe.* For example, if they have a MySpace.com page, they should keep it blocked to strangers. They can set it to be viewed by only people they know. Once information is put on the Internet, it can be copied and sent to anyone. Girls don't think that the provocative pictures they put on their Web site can be downloaded onto any predator's computer! Make sure the parent is listed as a friend so they can monitor the information on the Web page.

- ❉ *Challenge parents to keep computers in a family room or public area.* Most parents make the mistake of allowing their daughters to have a computer complete with a Web cam in their bedrooms. Most girls are not strong enough to resist the temptations that they will face.

- ❉ *Discuss the dangers of cell phones.* They provide safety for our daughters, but they are a growing problem in youth culture. Many students have cell phones and text message in church, youth group, and even during prayer time! Girls text each other constantly and will say things in their texts that they would never say in person. Picture phones can be a menace as well. Students use them to shoot pictures of their friends in embarrassing situations. Soon those pictures are spread to everyone, and the girl's reputation is on the line.

Packing Your Daughter's Suitcase for Life

When a baby girl is born, her parents begin packing a suitcase for their daughter's life. It is not a physical suitcase with clothes and toiletries, but it is a suitcase that will equip her for life as she becomes a young adult. The things packed in this suitcase will prepare her for marriage and parenthood. It will prepare her to become the woman God wants her to be. It is partly the church's responsibility to train parents how to pack a suitcase for their daughter. A good illustration to use in teaching parents about packing their daughter's suitcase is the following:

Has your mom or spouse ever packed a suitcase for you to go on a trip? Have you arrived at your hotel to find that you didn't have the things you needed but have things that you couldn't possibly use? Sometimes you can go to the store to get the needed items, but some of them are irreplaceable, like your worn out T-shirt that you prefer to wear to bed. As you look further in your suitcase, you think, "What was she thinking? I can't use my gloves and scarf. I'm in Miami!"

What are the things a girl will need when she walks out the door to live on her own? Parents begin when a baby is born by teaching her how to feed herself, go to the bathroom, dress herself, and take turns. As the girl grows older, parents continue to teach age-appropriate skills such as driving a car, setting up a bank account, managing money, filing taxes, and getting an apartment. Above all, she needs for her parents to pack understanding of how to love others, to be unselfish, to get rid of childish ways, to choose a godly husband, and to love the Lord God with all of her heart, mind, and soul.

Last, but most importantly, if parents are wise, they will teach girls to know when to take something out of the suitcase they don't need. Most of the things parents pack in their daughters' suitcases are packed by good example, but sometimes parents model the wrong things in front of their daughters. Churches can play an important role in teaching girls to discern good from evil. May God's Holy Spirit give our girls the discernment to know when to take the generational sin that has been passed down through their family and toss it out of the suitcase.

Parent ministry will not eliminate all of the mistakes parents make in raising their daughters, but it will lessen the difficulties. Churches and parents can partner together to raise up their daughters to be a new generation of godly women.

conclusion

Principles for a Successful Girls' Ministry

W HEN YOU BEGIN a girls' ministry, it will take time to grow a strong ministry in your church. You will try things that don't work, and you will try things that work well. It is important to remember to not give up when you feel an event isn't as effective as it could be. Longevity is important in girls' ministry.

It takes time to build a strong ministry of any kind. When a minister joins the staff of a new church, it has been my observation that it takes at least five years to build relationships and a ministry in that church. Often ministers do not stay long enough to build a successful ministry. When I joined the staff at First Baptist Church in Spartanburg, South Carolina, my pastor asked me to devise a five year plan for girls' ministry. That let me know that he expected me to be there for at least that long! I gave him a one-page plan that implemented the following principles:

Orientation

When beginning a girls' ministry, it is wise to spend the first year in observation. Acquaint yourself with existing programs to see if the needs of girls are already being partially met in other programs. You will learn about existing ministries and become familiar with ways you can enhance what it is already being done to minister to girls. You will begin to develop and foster relationships with women who are leaders and potential leaders. You will begin to develop relationships with girls by learning their names, remembering their birthdays, ministering to them when they have a need, and attending events that are important to them. It is also wise to meet with the youth minister and/or pastor to find out exactly what is expected from you. Keep the lines of communication open with him. Looking at the big picture and sizing it up is important in the first year of ministry.

Experimentation

As you become acquainted with the existing ministries, pray about new ideas and events that will meet the needs of teenage girls. Ask God to show you what events and ministry ideas will be appropriate for the girls in your church. You have to look for where He is working and join Him.

For example, a couple of moms in our church began a prayer breakfast for the cheerleaders at one of the local high schools. My immediate response was, "How can I be involved?" I asked the mom who was hosting the breakfast in her home if she needed me to come and help. She already had the help she needed and had a woman from another church there to speak every Friday morning. The moms were taking turns bringing breakfast and cleaning up afterward. She simply said, "You can pray for us." At first, I felt a little let down, but I soon realized that I had a great opportunity to pray for this group. I got a list of the names of the cheerleaders, and I pray for them by name each week. Our church donated Bibles to each girl recently, and in a few weeks I plan to take gift bags with goodies in them along with my card and a note saying that I am praying for them. God may not always be working the way or even where you imagined, but you should still pray for creative ways to do ministry. Experiment. Keep the things that work. You may plan an event or implement an idea that will be a total failure. Don't give up! You may need to fine-tune or even eliminate the event and try a different direction in the future.

Evaluation

Evaluation of events immediately afterward is important. Get feedback from girls, parents, and girls' ministry leaders. Make notes of things that need to be changed or improved at the next event. Evaluation is an important aspect of building a strong ministry. When someone gives you constructive criticism, ask yourself: *Is what she said true? If so, what do I need to do to fix the problem? If what she is saying is not true, how can I graciously work around her criticism and keep a good relationship with her?* Always work for a win-win situation. Sometimes, that is not possible due to the other person's unwillingness to work with you, but you should do your part to work out the situation to the benefit of everyone.

If you are simply doing an event to fill up the calendar, you are not conducting a successful ministry. Do not feel bad if you simply stop doing something that is not fulfilling the purpose and mission statement of your girls' ministry.

Implementation

Through trial and error, you will begin to see what is not working and what is successful in the girls' ministry in your church. When something is successful, you will want to implement that program or ministry and continue revising it to make it strong.

Multiplication

Starting small, deciding what works, and building on that is important. You may start with one or two women in your church who have a vision to minister to teenage girls. When other women begin to see the results of the ministry, they will want to be involved as well. You may plan an event and have only a small percentage of the girls in your church attend. If it is an event that is planned with excellence, is fun, and meets a need for teenage girls, then more girls will show up for the next event. You may start out with one special event the first year and build on that event for the next year. When you begin a mentoring and discipleship program, girls will talk, and eventually more girls will want to be involved as well. When you encourage girls to reach out to others, then your ministry will begin to multiply.

Acceleration

In time you will begin to figure out what works. As you fine tune the ministry for teenage girls in your church, more girls will get involved. At that point you will begin to accelerate in ministry. This may not occur until the third, fourth, or maybe even fifth year. You will develop relationships with women leaders, learn the strengths and weaknesses of those women, and begin to utilize them according to their strengths. You will develop relationships with teenage girls, and they will know that you are committed to them and your ministry to them. They will learn that you and the other women in the girls' ministry are there for them when they need you. More girls will become involved, and they will soon look forward to the special events and ministry that is happening. The girls who were in seventh grade when your ministry began will be upperclassmen at this point. Because you have trained them to become leaders, they will be reaching out to younger girls and bringing them along as well. Girls' ministry will begin to accelerate!

Celebration

In your heart, you will be able to celebrate the fact that as the girls' ministry is growing, you are seeing girls grow into godly young women. You may want to have a special event to celebrate the anniversary of your girls' ministry with girls giving their testimonies. When girls hear what God has been doing in the lives of other girls, they will want to be involved. Your celebration will probably be short-lived because there is much work to do, and it is never ending. You should gaze at God and glance at the success of your ministry.

I have experienced the celebration, but I have also experienced the down time when you feel like you are not successful in ministry. It seems that during those times, God always sends someone to encourage me. During the past month, I have had three young women come back to thank me for the part I played in their lives as teenage girls. These young women have grown to be godly young wives, mothers, and women. I took only a moment to celebrate the success of the ministry. There is still so much work to do. There are many girls in need, and God is working all around you. It's time to join Him in growing a new generation of women!

May God pour out His richest blessings as you seek God's will in ministry to teenage girls in your church and community. I look forward to partnering with you as we work together to grow the next generation of godly young women.

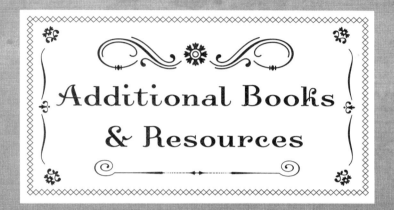

Additional Books
& Resources

Books

Adams, Chris. *Women Reaching Women: Beginning and Growing a Women's Ministry,* Nashville, TN: LifeWay Press, 1997, revised 2005.

Bennett, Tammy. *Looking Good from the Inside Out.* Grand Rapids, MI: Baker House-Fleming H. Revell, 2002.

Courtney, Vicki. *His Girl.* Nashville, TN: LifeWay Press, 2006.

Courtney, Vicki. *Your Girl: A Bible Study for Mothers of Teens.* Nashville, TN: LifeWay Press, 2006.

Courtney, Vicki. *TeenVirtue: Real Issues, Real Life...A Teen Girl's Survival Guide.* Nashville, TN: Broadman and Holman, 2005.

Courtney, Vicki. *TeenVirtue 2: A Teen Girl's Guide to Relationships.* Nashville, TN: Broadman and Holman, 2006

Courtney, Vicki. *Yada Yada: A Devotional Journal for Moms.* Nashville, TN: Broadman and Holman, 2004.

Cruse, Sheryle. *Thin Enough: My Spiritual Journey Through the Living Death of an Eating Disorder.* Birmingham, Alabama: New Hope Publishers, 2006.

Davis, Jimmie L. *Virtual You: Love, Beauty, Relationships, Purity, Truth.* Ventura, CA: Servant Publications, 2002.

DiMarco, Haley. *Mean Girls: Facing Your Beauty Turned Beast.* Grand Rapids, MI: Revell Publishing, 2004.

DiMarco, Haley. *Sexy Girls: How Hot is too Hot?* Grand Rapids, MI: Revell Publishing, 2006.

Dockrey, Karen. *The Youth Worker's Guide to Creative Bible Study.* Nashville, TN: Broadman and Holman, 1999.

Feldhahan, Shaunti and Lisa A. Rice. *For Young Women Only.* Sisters, OR: Multnomah Publishers, 2006.

George, Elizabeth. *A Young Woman After God's Own Heart.* Eugene, OR: Harvest House Publishers, 2002.

Gibbons, Casey Hartley. *A Girl's Life with God.* Birmingham, AL: New Hope Publishers, 2003.

Gibbs, Pam. *Designed By God: Answers to Students' Questions About Homesexuality.* Nashville, TN: LifeWay Press, 2004.

Hersh, Sharon. *Mom, I Feel Fat!: Becoming Your Daughter's Ally in Developing a Healthy Body Image.* Colorado Springs, CO: Focus on the Family, 2001.

Lewis, Carole and Cara Symank. *The Mother-Daughter Legacy.* Ventura, CA: Regal Books, 2004.

McDowell, Josh. *Handbook on Counseling Youth: A Comprehensive Guide for Equipping Youth Workers, Pastors, Teachers, Parents.* Nashville, TN: Word Publishing, 1995.

✓Musick, Helen, Dan Jessup, and Crystal Kirgiss. *Girls: 10 Gutsy, God Centered Sessions on Issues that Matter to Girls.* Grand Rapids, MI: Youth Specialities, 2002.

Olson, Ginny. *Teenage Girls: Exploring Issues Adolescent Girls Face and Strategies to Help Them.* Grand Rapids, MI: Youth Specialties, 2006.

✓Point of Grace. *Girls of Grace: Devotional and Bible Study Workbook.* West Monroe, LA: Howard Publishing Co., 2002.

✓Point of Grace. *Make It Real: Words, Worth, Relationships, and Me.* West Monroe, LA: Howard Publishing, 2005.

Prosperi, Whitney. *Girls Ministry 101.* Grand Rapids, MI: Zondervan: Youth Specialties, 2006.

Thomas, Angela. *Wild About You.* Nashville, TN: LifeWay Press, 2005.

White, Joe and Jim Weidmann, eds. *Parents' Guide to the Spiritual Mentoring of Teens.* Wheaton, IL: Tyndale House Publishers, 2001.

Internet Resources

www.briomag.com
www.cpyu.org
www.girlsofgrace.com
www.lifeway.com/students
www.onemillionmoms.com
www.onemillionyouth.com
www.onemilliondads.com
www.placeministries.org
www.truelovewaits.com
www.virtuousreality.com
www.youthministry.com

Notes

Chapter 1: Why Begin a Girls' Ministry?

1. ©2006 by Charles Montaldo. (http://crime.about.com/od/murder/p/ squeaky.htm)Used with permission of About, Inc. which can be found online at www.about.com. All rights reserved.
2. Ron Hutchcraft, *The Battle for a Generation* (1996; Chicago: Moody Press), 22.
3. Victor C. Strasburger, "Teen Pregnancy Rates in the USA," Coolnurse.com, http://www.coolnurse.com/teen_pregnancy_rates.htm.
4. Adolescent Medicine Committee, Canadian Paediatric Society, "Eating disorders in adolescents: principles of diagnosis and treatment," *Paediatrics and Child Health* 3(3) (1998): 189-92.
5. The National Campaign to Prevent Teen Pregnancy, "General Facts and Stats," teenpregnancy.org, http://www.teenpregnancy.org/resources/data/ genlfact.asp.
6. Centers for Disease Control and Prevention, "Sadness and suicide ideation and attempts" *Youth Risk Behavior Surveillance System: CDC Surveillance Summaries* 49, no. SS-5 (2001), 1-94.
7. "Teen Dating Violence," Coolnurse.com, http://www.coolnurse.com/dating_ violence.htm.
8. Orlando Sentinel, "Teen drinking: A serious health risk," Health Check: The Blog, 28 March 2006, http://blogs.orlandosentinel.com/features_ healthblog/2006/03/is_your_teen_on.html.

Chapter 2: What Are the Needs of Teen Girls?

1. Leonard Sweet, *Postmodern Pilgrims*, (2000; Nashville: Broadman and Holman Publishers), xxi.
2. Josh McDowell and Bob Hostetler, *Right from Wrong*, (1994; Dallas: Word Publishing), 16.
3. Josh McDowell and Bob Hostetler, *Beyond Belief to Conviction*, (2002; Wheaton, Ill.: Tyndale House Publishing), 15.
4. Ibid.
5. "The Asset Approach: Giving Kids What They Need to Succeed," Search Institute, http://www.unitedwaysb.org/assetapp.pdf#search=%22research%2 0on%20children%20need%20boundaries%22.

6. Forum on Child and Family Statistics, "America's Children in Brief: Key National Indicators of Well-Being, 2006—Family Structure and Children's Living Arrangements," ChildStats.gov, http://www.childstats. gov/americaschildren/pop6.asp#pop6a.

7. "Domestic Violence Facts," Sable House, http://www.open.org/sable/dvfacts.htm.

8. HIV/AIDS Surveillance Report 2004, vol. 16, Centers for Disease Control and Prevention, (2005, Atlanta: US Department of Health and Human Services), 1-46 and http://www.cdc.gov/hiv/topics/surveillance/resources/reports/2004report/pdf/2004SurveillanceReport.pdf.

9. The National Women's Health and Information Center, "Menstruation and the Menstrual Cycle," U.S. Department of Health and Human Services: womenshealth.gov, http://forwoman.org/faq/menstru.htm.

Chapter 3: What Is Girls' Ministry?

1. Bill and Pam Farrel, *Men Are like Waffles-Women Are like Spaghetti: Understanding and Delighting in Your Differences*, (2001; Eugene, Ore.: Harvest House Publishers), 11.

2. Ibid, 13.

Chapter 4: A Team Approach in Beginning Girls' Ministry

1. "Our Purpose," Whitesburg Baptist Church, (Huntsville, Ala.) http://www. wbccares.org/girls/purpose.html.

2. "twentyfourseven: Girls Ministry," Student Ministry of First Baptist Church of Springdale, Arkansas, http://www.247nwa.com/springdale/php/girls.php.

3. "About Girl's Ministry," Quail Springs Church of Christ (Oklahoma City, Okla.), http://quailchurch.com/cgi-bin/NewsList.cgi?section=high&cat=Girl's%20Ministry&rec=380.

4. "The Becoming — HS Girls' Ministry," Calvary Church (Santa Ana, Calif.), http://www.calvarylife.org/connect/TheBecoming.html.

Chapter 5: Developing and Training Leadership

1. *The Hebrew-Greek Key Study Bible*, (1996; Chattanooga, Tenn.: AMG Publishers), 1633.

2. Knute Larson, "Titus," *Holman New Testament Commentary*, (2000; Nashville: Broadman and Holman Publishing), 360.

CHAPTER 6: SMALL GROUP DISCIPLESHIP & MENTORING

1. Ginny Olson, *Teenage Girls: Exploring Issues Adolescent Girls Face and Strategies to Help Them*, (2006; Gand Rapids, Mich.: Zondervan Publishers), 9.

2. Peter S. Bearman, "Promising the Future: Virginity Pledges and First Intercourse," *American Journal of Sociology* 106, no. 4 (2001), 859.

3. Knute Larson, ""Titus," *Holman New Testament Commentary*, (2000; Nashville: Broadman and Holman Publishing), 361.

4. John and Staci Eldredge, *Captivating: Unveiling the Mystery of a Woman's Soul*, (2005; Nashville: Thomas Nelson Publishers), 31-32.

5. "20 USC 4071: The Equal Access Act," U.S. Department of Justice, http://www.usdoj.gov/crt/cor/byagency/ed4071.htm.

CHAPTER 7: SPECIAL EVENTS FOR TEENAGE GIRLS

1. John and Staci Eldredge, *Captivating: Unveiling the Mystery of a Woman's Soul*, (2005; Nashville: Thomas Nelson Publishers), 8.

CHAPTER 8: COUNSELING ISSUES WITH TEENAGE GIRLS

1. Jacqueline Kirby Wilkins, "Single-parent Families in Poverty," The Ohio State University, http://www.hec.ohio-state.edu/famlife/bulletin/volume.1/bullart1.htm and Paul R. Amato, "Children's adjustment to divorce: Theories, hypotheses, and empirical support," *Journal of Marriage and the Family*, 55 (1993): 23-58.

2. *Dorland's Medical Dictionary*, s.v. "physical abuse," 30th ed. (2003; Philadelphia: WB Saunders).

3. "Child Neglect and Abuse," Merck Manual Home Edition, http://www.merck.com/mmhe/sec23/ch288/ch288a.html.

4. National Center for PTSD, "Child Sexual Abuse," United States Department of Veterans Affairs, http://www.ncptsd.va.gov/facts/specific/fs_child_sexual_abuse.html.

5. Adam M. Tomison, "Update on Child Sexual Abuse," National Child Protection Clearinghouse, http://www.aifs.gov.au/nch/issues5.html.

6. "Statistics Surrounding Child Sexual Abuse," Darkness to Light, http://www.darkness2light.org/KnowAbout/statistics_2.asp.

7. Carrie Wiatt, interview by WebMD Live, WebMD.com, July 5, 2005, http://webmd.com/content/chat_transcripts/1/108783.htm?printing=true.

8. Linda Smolak, *National Eating Disorders Association/Next Boor Neighbors Puppet Guide Book*, 1996.

9. Dianne Neumark-Sztainer, *I'm, Like, SO Fat!: Helping Your Teen Make Healthy Choices about Eating and Exercise in a Weight Obsessed World* (2005; New York: The Guilford Press), 5.

10. Victor C. Strasburger, "Teen Pregnancy Rates in the USA," Coolnurse.com, http://www.coolnurse.com/teen_pregnancy_rates.htm.

11. Darroch JE and Singh S, "Why is Teenage Pregnancy Declining? the roles of abstinence, sexual activity and contraceptive use," *Occasional Report*, New York: Guttmacher Institute, 1999, No. 1.

12. STD Surveillance 2003, "Trends in Reportable Sexually Transmitted Diseases in the United States 2003—National Data on Chlamydia, Gnorrhea and Syphilis," Centers for Disease Control and Prevention, http://www.cdc.gov/std/stats03/trends2003.htm#1.

13. Oswald Chambers, "June 25," *My Utmost for His Highest* (Grand Rapids, MI: Discovery House Publishers, 1992).

14. "Rainbow party (sexuality)," Wikipedia, http://en.wikipedia.org/wiki/Rainbow_party_(sexuality).

15. Laura Sessions Stepp, "Partway Gay?," washingtonpost.com, http://www.washingtonpost.com/ac2/wp-dyn/A53140-2004Jan4?language=printer.

16. Ibid.

17. "Parents Can Make a Real Difference in Protecting Teens from Alcohol," The Desert Sun, July 21, 2006, www.thedesertsun.com.

18. Ibid.

19. NIH Publication No. 00-3561: "Depression," National Institute of Mental Health, http://www.nimh.nih.gov/publicat/depression.cfm#ptdep3.

20. Deb Martinson, "Self-Injury," Focus Adolescent Services, http://www.focusas.com/SelfInjury.html.

21. "Self-harm," Wikipedia, http://en.wikipedia.org/wiki/Self-harm.

22. Ibid.

23. Ibid.

CHAPTER 9: MINISTRY TO PARENTS OF TEEN GIRLS

1. Spirituality in Higher Education, "College Students Show High Levels of Spiritual and Religious Engagement," Higher Education Research Institute, University of California, Los Angeles, http://spirituality.ucla.edu/news/2003-11-21.html.

2. "Fathers Are Power!ful: Research and Statistics" Girl Power!, http://www.girlpower.gov/adultswhocare/fathers/stats.htm.

3. Mark D. Regnerus and Laura B. Luchies, "The Parent-Child Relationship and Opportunities for Adolescents' First Sex," *Journal of Family Issues* 27 (February 2006): 131-158.

4. Stephanie M. Bowling and Ronald J. Werner-Wilson, "How Does the Relationship Between Fathers and Daughters Influence the Sexual Behavior and Attitudes of Heterosexual Adolescent Females?," http://www.public.iastate.edu/~rwwilson/ncfr-98.pdf.

5. The Faith Journey of Young Adults, "A glimpse at the role of faith in the lives of young adults (ages 18-30)," Student Leadership Training Network, http://www.sltn.com/FJYA/Study/quant_findings.htm.

6. Vicki Courtney, *Your Girl: Raising a Godly Daughter in an Ungodly World.* (2004; Nashville: Broadman and Holman Publishers), 178.